Secrets to Tame a Mystical Dragon

Sharron Gleason, CMT, TTT

Published by
Conscious Media Publishing
New York, NY 10022

Copyright © 2017 by Sharron Gleason

All rights reserved. No part of this book may be reproduced or transmitted in any form or by in any means, electronic or mechanical, including photocopying, recording, or by any information storage and retrieval system, without the written permission of the Publisher, except where permitted by law.

Names and places have been changed in this book. While the accuracy of the story and countries have remained true, it was necessary in some instances to alter city names and personal names to protect identities.

Trauma Touch Healing (TTH) is a trademarked therapy created and founded by Sharron Gleason.

Manufactured in the United States of America, or in the United Kingdom when distributed elsewhere.

Gleason, Sharron
    Secrets to Tame a Mystical Dragon
    LCCN: 2017947575
    ISBN:
    Paperback: 978-1-941595-00-8
    eBook: 978-1-941595-01-5

Cover design: Joe Potter
Interior design: Claudia Volkman

www.traumatouchhealing.com

Table of Contents

Dedication...5
What Is a Trauma Touch Healer?..7
Prologue..9
Introduction...11
One: My Life Zero to Eleven Years Old..19
Two: My Life Eleven to Twenty-Three Years Old................................29
Three: Healing a Shattered Soul..49
Four: What Is Trauma Touch Healing? A Vital Missing Link Explained........73
Five: Cracking the PTSD Code!
    The Positive Effects of Trauma Touch Healing................................89
Six: What Is Dissociation?...113
Seven: Re-creating Lost Boundaries..119
Eight: Finding Joy and Youthful Free Spirit Again!..........................123
Nine: The Emotional Release Process...127
Ten: Ego: The Enemy of Healing..141
Eleven: Trauma Healing within Mainstream/Alternative Medicine—
    What Is Wrong?..151
Epilogue..159
About the Author...169
Bibliography...171

Dedication

For my little brother Matthew, to whom I was a mother figure. I protected him, while he gave me his unconditional love and trust. I am so sorry, Matthew, that I could not ultimately protect you. I was just too young and inexperienced myself, despite my best intentions.

What Is a Trauma Touch Healer?

"What work do you do?" I am asked.

"I'm a Trauma Touch Healer," I say.

To this answer I get the usual reply, "What is a Trauma Touch Healer?"

This is one of the reasons I wrote this book—to educate more people on what this amazing therapy is and what its benefits are for trauma survivors and those suffering the effects of Post Traumatic Stress Disorder, or PTSD. I also hope to encourage more practitioners to learn its unique, cutting edge, organic methods.

It's true. The issues are in the tissues!

Trauma Touch Healing is a new unique and organic 12-week trauma release therapy designed by the author. It combines Trauma Touch Therapy, Trauma Intervention, and Emotional 911 techniques which control stress, triggers, and symptoms of PTSD. Further information can be obtained from the TTH website at www.traumatouchhealing.com.

Prologue

A Seaside City in South Africa

I opened my eyes at 5.30 a.m. in the beautiful white room at the top of the house where I was temporarily living. The hot, summer African sun was just rising over the Indian Ocean—a huge, beautiful, orange ball that I could see through the big glass windows in front of me.

While I sleepily watched, I slowly became aware of a silhouette of the treetop in my view where two birds clung expertly, moving in perfect synchronicity as the branches swayed to gentle ocean breezes. I lay fascinated, watching them while contemplating getting up and making my first cup of tea for the day.

I was in this room to begin writing my book. The journey to this point seemed enormously long. For several years, the pages were being written in my head, and now, at long last, here I was. I felt ripe—ready to release the essential words that needed to be expressed, excited at the prospect that my discoveries could really improve so many lives for the better, as they had for me.

For those who have been through a trauma of any kind, the words in this book may make the difference from merely surviving to thriving, despite the trauma. It is a story of my own traumatic past and of the long, determined personal journey of healing from it—how I ultimately discovered Trauma Touch Healing and, in doing so, finally found a therapy that really presented me with the opportunity and practical tools to control and permanently tame a very fierce mystical dragon—PTSD.

Introduction

In preparation for the writing of this book, I read many books regarding other people's personal accounts of trauma, what they had endured, and how this affected them. In both treating survivors and after reading the many personal accounts, it cannot be emphasized enough how similar we react to trauma no matter what the actual trauma is. A common survivor consequence over time, especially with severe trauma, is a condition called Post Traumatic Stress Disorder, also known as PTSD. I have discovered that, in general, this is a vastly misunderstood condition, which results in those who suffer with it being very poorly directed for treatment.

There is, of course, plenty of information about this complicated condition in the medical world, but to date, nobody seems to have pieced this information together as a cohesive whole to present to a trauma survivor, thereby giving that person a helpful pathway to healing and recovering. This is due, in my opinion, to three very important components: misunderstanding the individual and misdiagnosing manifestations within their physical, mental, and emotional/spiritual bodies of how their bodies react to trauma; unhelpful, inflated egos of practitioners; and often the complete lack in ethics of so-called "healers" who are often more concerned about lining their pockets than helping their clients/patients.

In the following chapters, I will discuss these three components in more detail. For now, I must mention that one of the great confusions of trauma is that while as human beings with physical bodies we react to a traumatic event in similar fashion (fight-or-flight response), how we react as emotional beings is something entirely different and unique from one another. You may have two or more persons who experience the same trauma—a car accident, for example—but several months later they are experiencing the aftereffects quite differently. One may become extremely angry, another may find himself suffering from depression, and yet another has become very fearful and is experiencing high levels of anxiety. Why is this? Why do we respond so differently to the same given traumatic event?

I believe this is a key to the reason that, so far, we have not been very effective in helping those suffering from trauma and PTSD to recover from their traumatic pasts. In addition to being physical beings, at our core we are first and foremost energetic beings. Our energetic self is separate and connected to our physical self and gives it life. As energetic beings, we are born and blueprinted very differently from each other. We are all unique—something like fingerprints.

As gross physical beings, we are born the same—one heart, two lungs, two kidneys etc.—and each has its own predictable system of operation the same as other human beings. However, the emotional or energetic body of each individual responds individually and uniquely to traumatic events. It is important to see this. While we treat the physical body, the emotional body needs a completely different kind of treatment.

At the physical level, our emotional, energetic body is tied closely to the neurological system of the body. This neurological system responds directly to trauma of any kind. Within the brain this system is called the limbic system, which controls the primitive/emotional center. During a traumatic event, the limbic system responds by going into fight-or-flight mode, immediately sending down into the body various chemicals, such as adrenalin, which prepares the body, muscles, and other tissues to fight or flee to preserve life.

Because of the sheer number of super fast electrical charges shot into the body through this response, the body's electrical system can actually be overwhelmed if trauma is sustained long enough, severely enough, or repetitively enough. Too much electrical "heat" alters this delicate system just the same as an electrical surge will fry a plugged-in computer or an electrical box will short-circuit due to too much energy overload.

The fight-or-flight response was not designed to be a sustained response, but rather a short-term emergency solution for the body to preserve life in a life-threatening situation. So what happens when this system is forced by circumstance to stay continuously open, freezing and remaining sustained in fight-or-flight for long periods of time as experienced during repeated abuse

Introduction

or war trauma or in chronic PTSD? Obviously, there must be negative ramifications. This question is discussed later in the book.

One way to relieve this system is to release the electrical charges out of the body immediately after a traumatic event. Humans, unfortunately, are not very good at doing this. Because so much overwhelming emotion is experienced during trauma, we go into a natural fear mode causing us to freeze, hold, and lock these charges in the body instead of releasing them. If enough of these charges are held in the body, this negative energy starts to accumulate in the cells and ultimately begins to overwhelm the body's ability to maintain homeostasis (natural balance). Progressively, if this negativity and unbalance is sustained long enough in the body tissue, it can become physically symptomatic by eventually manifesting itself as a disease (*dis*-ease) or other chronic conditions.

Herein lies the first problem of the long-term effects of trauma. By treating a chronic physical ailment or a disease, you may be merely treating a symptom of a deeper, quantum-level emotional problem. By doing so, you cannot be really effective in healing the person. To help in the healing process, we must also begin to look at the bigger picture and examine the *root cause* of the physical symptoms the patient may be exhibiting. If we are to become effective healers with trauma survivors, we cannot afford the simplistic approach of always looking at the tip of the iceberg while conveniently ignoring the much larger body of ice hidden under the water.

For starters, in any intake of a patient/client with disease or chronic symptoms, questions should also be asked about any history of trauma. Often people don't realize or connect the dots that their past trauma backgrounds are even having an impact on their physical health today! Who should they learn this from? It is our duty as healers to become as educated as possible in these cases to inform our clients to at least examine this. While the body is being treated by a physician, a patient/client can also simultaneously be taught how to release all the accumulated negative energy from the body tissue under the care of another therapist. This will definitely expedite the healing process.

We know that trauma is recorded in each cell of the body at the microbiological level. This energy can and must be released from each cell before the neurological/emotional/electrical blueprint can correct itself and begin to heal. From this *root cause* emotional release healing, trauma begins to reverse itself out of the body. This is really possible! When it reverses itself, negative emotional, mental, and physical symptoms naturally begin to correct and heal. There is an old saying in the bodyworkers' world that "the issues are in the tissues." To help release these emotional issues, you must go to a practitioner who is trained and qualified to do this particular, specialized work.

There are three aspects to trauma—physical, mental, and emotional/spiritual. There may or may not be physical damage from the event, but if there is physical damage, first and foremost it is a physician who must help you. Once the initial physical healing is complete, it is essential that a psychologist who specializes in trauma be consulted so you can gain some balance and understanding of what has happened to you, talk about the event, and discuss the various issues that trouble you. This process may last and satisfy you for only a few months. Trust yourself when you feel you have had enough and the psychologist cannot help you anymore, and tell them so. Time and again I meet clients who have been treated for years and years even though they had long felt that the psychologist was no longer helpful. Yet, week after week, month after month, year after year, the appointments were set while they became more despondent and depressed because they believed their lack of improvement meant something was wrong with *them*. Also, by this time the trauma has had all the time in the world to coil itself more deeply into the body tissue, and PTSD is now chronic and manifesting in very negative physical ways. Still, the psychologist is often not referring the patient to somebody who could be more effective at this stage. It must be said that in trauma there is no one modality that is the silver bullet. Each has its limits and maximum scope in healing a client.

In my opinion, after the psychologist, your next step should be a certified Trauma Touch Healer who will help with special breathing techniques to calm the limbic system, teach you how to prevent triggering and subsequent dissociation, reestablish and reclaim boundaries (real techniques, not simply talking about it), give techniques to quickly counteract depression, as well as show how to release negative emotions from the body during actual, hands-on release work during the body sessions. It is an intense, narrow modality that is highly focused on trauma healing and highly effective as a result. This process will usually take you eleven weeks (a small percentage of clients may need more therapy). Upon completion, the Trauma Touch Healer can guide you to which bodyworker can best help you navigate the next stages of healing according to your unique needs.

Introduction

Doesn't this process make more sense on your road to healing? Isn't it better to have a clear, helpful, and effective pathway to recovering from trauma instead of bumbling along blindly, getting zero help from physicians and psychologists or alternative healers who would have you believe that being treated by them alone will help you? Or physicians and psychologists simply remaining so ignorant of other modalities relating to trauma that they do not even know whom to refer you to?

It is my personal and observation experience that going to bodyworkers who are not specifically trained in trauma is very counterproductive and often very harmful. Once emotional release work has been completed, there are many practitioners out there who can be very helpful with residual physical problems caused by trauma and stress. However, I have had so many calls from people who were advised to see a massage therapist or chiropractor, and while these practitioners were working with them, they experienced unexpected, spontaneous emotional releases. With trauma survivors, often just a touch in a particular place can trigger a spontaneous release. If a practitioner has not done a broad enough information-gathering intake with a client and is therefore unaware of his or her status as a trauma survivor, or if there is insufficient or no prior training in trauma responses and the emotional releasing is not being done in a safe, slow, controlled way, then an emotional release is counterproductive. A chaotically unwinding emotional release is frightening to both client and practitioner. If combined with dissociation, it is actually harmful. The client has now been re-victimized and re-traumatized. (This will be discussed later.) As well-meaning as you may be as a healer, a lack of proper training in the emotional aspects of healing trauma has just further damaged your client, and it is very doubtful he/she will ever return to you for further treatment. They will not feel safe with you. And rightfully so!

The most safe and caring way that I know to help a trauma survivor is by following the steps above: Firstly, a physician (if needed) for healing the body and who may also refer you to a specialist or physical or occupational therapist, etc. Secondly, the psychologist (and/or psychiatrist if needed) to give much needed balance and understanding of the traumatic event. (Both should be specialized in the treatment of trauma). Thirdly, a Trauma Touch Healer who is specialized to help safely and slowly release negative emotional trauma out of the tissues of the body and who will also give very helpful, practical techniques to cope with emotional symptoms of trauma.

After completing these initial steps, it is then highly beneficial to begin to discover other healing techniques and modalities that may help you on your own, unique pathway to healing. Some examples of bodyworkers include acupuncturists, chiropractors, massage therapists, cranial-sacral therapists, yoga instructors, and energy workers of all kinds. Once negative energy is released from the body tissue, the body clears and begins to dialogue with you again and telling you what it needs. In this way, I am always confident that after completing Trauma Touch Healing treatments, a client will gravitate naturally towards the next therapist most needed for the next step in healing.

So, dear reader, a smorgasbord of information awaits you in the following pages. To the confused (that has been most of us), I say just bear with me. Read on, and you will begin to understand. For those who doubt, read on with an open mind. To those who read and say, "Yes! This is what I have been looking for," do not hesitate to grab onto the rope that is extended to you to extricate yourself from the deep, dark hole we trauma survivors know so well! When your need for healing is stronger than your fear, it is your fighting spirit and readiness that is prevailing. When you are finally ready to surrender, let go of the past and release yourself for transformation, bravely considering taking the great leap of faith off a very high cliff despite your fears, it is here where you will discover your greatest healing.

The journey is rough, and the necessary learning is vast, but the desperate seeking for wholeness and empowerment again feeds the soul and expands the mind to places others know not. Through trauma, we are catapulted far out of the box to foreign regions of new feelings and emotions where we are often forced to experience a daily diet of anxiety, fear, depression, sadness, triggering, dissociation, lack of empowerment, and boundaries. Often we do not recognize ourselves post-trauma and begin to perceive (correctly) that our negative condition gains strength over time instead of weakening. Some of us become comfortable with our new self, stuck and frozen in fear and afraid to change or, worse, wanting to return to our former selves but not knowing the way back. To those survivors, please read on and believe. It is possible to heal.

For all the brave warriors, I say, gradually and with the correct therapies, together with willingness and a strong determination to heal, if you so choose, it is possible to not only survive but also emotionally recover and thrive again! My hope is that this book empowers you with critical healing

Introduction

knowledge of how to make your journey to recovery much faster, smoother, simpler, and easier to walk and understand. It is a pleasure to share my own long, personal journey of healing with you—an extraordinary sojourn I have been privileged to travel while learning and discovering the *Secrets to Tame a Mystical Dragon.*

I learned that courage was not the absence of fear, but the triumph over it. I felt fear myself more times than I can remember, but I hid it behind a mask of boldness. The brave man is not he who does not feel afraid, but he who conquers fear.

—Nelson Mandela, 1995

ONE

My Life Zero to Eleven Years Old

My early years were a harsh reality. I wished for the warm cuddles of a mother, the smell of cookies baking in a pretty kitchen, a beautiful garden with a swing, fragrant flowers, green grass to lie in, and a strong father who could keep us all intact. These wants and needs appealed to my hypersensitive nature, and the security I craved would have calmed me. What I got instead was something quite different. What I got molded my entire life and wounded me so deeply that I have spent a lifetime trying to heal from its effects, endeavoring along the way to find adequate healers to help me do so. I will share the journey of my healing adventures—some good, some bad. I will also share how, in time, I was inspired to become a specialized healer of trauma. Here is the story of my traumatic and dysfunctional childhood and my attempts to reverse the fallout from years of emotional abuse and neglect.

It is my hope that this sharing will open the eyes of parents everywhere and inspire them to seriously watch how they treat their children and realize how their actions affect the open heart of a child. It is also my hope that those who have gone through any traumatic experience that is impacting their lives and relationships in a negative way will be able to take this formula for healing and improve their own lives immeasurably!

Ultimately, I believe it is all about thriving in your life. It is about living life to its fullest potential for power, joy, and vitality and not just remaining stuck in a struggling survival mode due to something you had no control over in the first place. I would like to suggest that it is possible to reverse the negative effects of trauma. It is not easy, however; it takes great determination, many years of various therapies, and a great desire to overcome the fear of making that choice. It's challenging, but it is possible.

Through my own experience, research, and treatment of traumatized clients, I have identified a sound formula, which I believe, if followed, will shift your life positively beyond your belief! It must also be said that it is irrelevant what the particular trauma is that was experienced. For example, PTSD is common to any trauma survivor, regardless of whether one is a war veteran; rape survivor; accident survivor; witness of trauma; survivor of emotional, physical, or sexual abuse; victim/witness of a violent crime, battering, or surgical traumas; and so on. The formula will work for anybody who has experienced trauma and who is presently suffering from its aftereffects.

I really cannot recall any happy moments living in the little one-bedroom flat with my parents. It was a depressing atmosphere—small and cramped. I slept in a bedroom that had been created for me in an enclosed patio. I became very aware that my mother was not affectionate or warm toward me, and she seemed to really resent the affection my father and I held for each other. My father loved me, but I quickly realized as I grew up that I had a mother who was very jealous of our relationship. If my father and I spent any kind of quality time together, she was sure to interrupt our interaction by creating an unpleasant argument with him or separating us by demanding he go complete some chore. This repetitive, associative unpleasantness occurred whenever we attempted to be together. Sadly, it began to limit our closeness.

Of course, this was very confusing for a young child. It did not make me feel very loved or wanted by my mother. What was even more confusing was that my father, instead of challenging her on this, always surrendered to her in an attempt to keep the peace. This lack of challenge from my father further encouraged my mother's poor behavior, and she really became an uncontested tyrant within our family. As a result, constant fighting, squabbling, nagging, and criticizing were a part of our daily fare. Adding to this situation was the fact that these two people loved their social lives above all else. Drinking and partying were their priority—not their child.

I had already developed emotional problems during these early years. My aunt once told me about a time she visited us when I was around six months old. I was a cranky baby due to a later-discovered milk allergy. I was not breastfed but given a diet of cow's milk, which did not agree with me and made me a sick, thin baby who suffered from chronic colic and crying. My visiting aunt told me that she was shocked to discover my mother hitting and smacking me hard whenever I cried. My aunt had apparently asked my mother to stop doing this by pointing out that I was just a small baby. Clearly, my mother was clueless as to how to be a caring mother. But since my father did nothing to prevent this abusive behavior, he too was clueless as to how to be a father.

As an adult, I remember somebody asking me about my childhood. After hearing my response, the person replied, "Wow! Usually a child has one bad parent and the other good, who is capable of balancing the situation, but in your case, both were bad parents." I always felt that on an emotional level, I was in the hands of two very immature people. It felt dangerous and insecure. My welfare was not a priority.

As I got a little bigger, I remember always having a dripping nose, colds, acutely sore throats, and painful earaches. I also remember there simply was no relief from the constant fighting and discord in our family. My father, who should have been protective, often just looked the other way. On the rare occasions when he challenged my mother, our lives were made so miserable that it simply wasn't worth it.

I remember being force-fed at the little kitchen table. I hated the taste of green beans, and because of the way they were prepared, they scratched my throat as I ate them. Naturally, I always left them on my plate. My mother would then force-feed them to me and would not release me from the dining table until they were eaten. I remember throwing up the beans on more than one occasion, yet still she continued.

I remember asking my mother one time if she was my stepmother, because all the fairy tales told of horrible, unkind stepmothers who treated their children badly. I felt she surely could not be my real mother. A real mother would be kind and loving and warm, and that's definitely not what I was feeling from her. I remember being hit so hard in the head in response to that question that it knocked me sideways into the wall. All the while she yelled that she was, indeed, my mother.

My father was reckless. He was more like another child than a father. One time when I was three, he encouraged me to climb up the highest competition diving board at the local swimming pool and assured and convinced me that he would catch me in the water after I had jumped off. I nervously climbed up the long steps to the top and then looked down in fear at my father waiting to catch me. With his encouragement, I jumped. He missed me, and I dropped like a rock, plunging into the deep end of the pool. He had to dive under the water to bring me up from the bottom of the pool, as I was choking, coughing, and spluttering. He thought it was hilarious and laughingly congratulated me on my bravery! Heaven knows where my mother was during these events, but I don't remember any intervention.

On another occasion, my father was shaving in the bathroom. I was walking around the flat in my mother's high-heeled shoes. While I was watching him shave, somehow my father dropped the razor, which landed inside the large shoe I was wearing. It lodged itself behind my little heel and cut it badly. As I jumped in pain from the initial cut, the razor continued to slice into my skin. I remember lots of pain and lots of blood. Another time, he had made a wooden rocking horse for me. It had a horsehair tail attached by a hook, which he had failed to close and make safe. When I was rocking one day, I fell off the back of the horse, and the hook dug into my inner thigh, tearing the skin open. Again, there was a lot of blood.

With all this neglectful, irresponsible behavior, it was really just a matter of time before it became life-threatening. The following event convinced me, even at five, that I was in a situation I needed to disassociate from. My nasal/throat/ear condition had deteriorated to such a degree that I was taken to a doctor who diagnosed me with acute tonsillitis and suggested, even though I was very young, that my tonsils and adenoids should be removed. After the surgery and a short hospital stay, I was released to my parents and taken home.

One night, shortly after being released, I awoke at home feeling very nauseated and began to throw up. Scared, I remember crying for my parents as I choked and vomited in the completely dark flat. I quickly began to panic when nobody answered my cries for help, and I observed large, dark, sticky-feeling lumps all over my bed. All my instincts told me that something was very wrong, and I remember feeling terrified. What I didn't know was that I was in a fight for my life. The stitches in my throat had come loose, and I was hemorrhaging!

Thankfully, at that point, our downstairs neighbor and family friend, who was a registered nurse, heard me crying. She was aware that I had been hospitalized for a tonsillectomy. She and her husband ran upstairs and broke the glass in the front door to gain entry. When they realized I was alone, they quickly got ice from the refrigerator, wrapped it in a towel, and placed it on my throat to stanch the bleeding. After wrapping me in a blanket, they rushed me by car to a hospital where I was again taken to surgery to repair the damage. This husband and wife's quick thinking and actions had saved my life.

Where were my parents? At a party. Apparently, it wasn't important enough to ensure that I, at least, had a babysitter. I had been left alone to fend for myself, despite being recently discharged from the hospital for a surgery with a known history of stitches coming loose. My parents had to have been made aware of this by hospital staff. I was very lucky. Most children simply keep swallowing the blood as they sleep until they die. In my case, my sensitive stomach had thrown the blood up, signaling the potentially fatal situation. As an adult, I have often wondered how many times I had been left alone at home. Just by natural, protective instincts, it would have been inconceivable for me to leave my own children alone in a similar situation—or any situation, for that matter.

When I was almost six years old, we had already moved into a house nearby, and my baby brother, Matthew, was born. Till that point, I had lived the often lonely life of an only child, so I remember being very excited about his impending birth. When I first saw him after my mother returned from the hospital, I felt all the protective instincts of an older sister. I also remember feeling a great love for him. He was so incredibly cute with his chubby little legs and arms wiggling around.

But true to, and due to, our unhealthy family dynamics, as he started to grow up, he always seemed to experience some accident or other, especially as a toddler. I was attending school at this point, and he was left alone at home with my mother. I remember him being burned at some point and covered in bandages. Another time, he fell and cut his chin, which required an emergency room visit and stitches. I did witness one accident when an iron was left sitting on an ironing board with the plug hanging down onto the floor. He had crawled over to the cord and pulled on it. The iron came hurtling down with the sharp point first and hit him just below the eye. Again, there was lots of blood and stitches. Here was the pattern once again. One would think that at some point my parents would have "gotten it," but the dysfunctional behaviors continued—the friends, the parties, the drinking, and the neglect of their children. They were both just simply not in possession of any normal, mature, natural instinct to protect their young.

I am afraid that by that time, I too had picked up the bad habits of being oblivious of safety. I remember one occasion when my mother asked me to take care of my infant brother while he was in his pram. It was one of those large, old-fashioned prams with a carriage, large wheels, and one large handle. My mother wanted to spend time talking with a friend on the phone, so I had been instructed to watch my brother.

I sat on the wooden rail of our wrap-around verandah with my feet on the handle of the pram. He was fussy, so while I sat on the rail, I pushed the pram back and forth with my feet. Then I slipped, and as I did, my feet pushed down on the handle, and my poor brother was catapulted out of the pram. He landed on his head onto the hard tile verandah floor. It is no surprise then that my brother grew up in great fear.

When I was not around, he would not let my mother or father out of his sight. He simply could not be left alone. Even when my mother played tennis, she had to take him onto the tennis court with her, or he would become hysterical. He clung to my father whenever he was around, especially when in the company of other people. When I was home, I assumed the mother role, and more and more, my brother and I began to adopt an attitude of us against our parents and the world. We naturally began to form a very close bond, I believe, in an attempt to form some kind of security net around us for survival.

It must be said here that outwardly we looked well cared for. We were well dressed and well fed, and I am sure we looked like a normal family. My parents were very clever and talented in that way. For all public appearances, great attempts were made to make our family look as normal as possible. It was a huge charade that continued their entire lives. Inside it was sick, unhappy, dangerous, and highly dysfunctional—a disaster waiting to happen. It seemed to me that on a daily basis we experienced split and contrasting realities. Outside the home, all was happy and smiling and loving, but the moment we arrived home, the misery, fighting, and tearing apart began once again. For me, this was a very confusing phenomenon—a sort of "show time" mentality. It was as if our parents realized how bad it was, but they didn't know how or care enough to find the strength and courage to correct the situation. They found the perfect easy solution to their guilt by simply hiding it from friends, family, and the public at large. We were kind of play acting the perfect family. It was highly deceptive and dishonest, and being an intelligent child, I didn't trust it. From experience, my instincts clearly told me that in order to survive my life, self-sufficiency was the key.

When I was eight and my brother was two, my parents bought our first home. It was a small, three-bedroom, one-and-a-half bathroom house in a beautiful country neighborhood. Finally, I got what I always wanted—green grass, a huge rose garden, and lots of flowers and trees to play in. They even bought us a swing! I was well into the play acting by then, and this outward appearance of prettiness was therapeutic and definitely took the edge off. It enabled me to escape all the truth and ugliness of our family dynamics.

Inside, things were spinning out of control. I do remember at this time that the drinking and the partying were escalating and taking a toll on our family. There were attempts at some normalcy, but they were very erratic. I remember my drunk mother often stumbling around the kitchen trying to get dinner ready before my father returned from work. We didn't dare talk to her, or the screaming would start. We stayed out of the way. When she was like this, my father would get angry when he returned from work. Inevitably, an argument would erupt, and the screaming would start again. I felt we children were constantly walking on eggshells, never knowing what would erupt at any given moment. This constant tension was very stressful and kept us on high alert. Then something awful happened.

One day my mother just didn't return home. It turns out she had run off with the husband of one of the women from the tennis club. My father was left devastated with two small children. My grandmother came to help him with us when he was at work and moved into our house from her home very far away. I used to listen to my father crying at night, and I really hated my mother for that! It was so disrupting for all of us. And then, just when we were returning to some kind of routine, she showed up on our doorstep again. Apparently, the romance hadn't worked out, and she wanted my father to take her back. And he did. I cannot swear that she repeated this, but I seem to distantly remember that she did this a second time. Again, he took her back. By this time, I had lost all respect for him—and her. I do remember asking her one day why she had returned to us. She told me that she was not going to lose out on my father's pension money and benefits and that if they divorced she would lose access to this future security. There was no mention of having missed me, my brother, or my father.

I was slowly divorcing myself emotionally from my parents, because it just didn't seem safe to rely on either one of them any more than was necessary. I loved to play tennis and spent all my spare time playing. It was therapeutic. When I was playing tennis, I could focus on the game and escape the miserable realities of my home life. I delved into it competitively and excelled at it. Winning matches made me feel strong, happy, and in control of my life. So I won a lot!

As a family, we were spinning out of control and always seemed to be hanging on to the threads of a deteriorating fabric. It was a fabric that was so weak, threadbare, and fragile that it felt like any small pull in any direction would surely tear it asunder. The inevitable finally happened one awful night. It was huge and descended upon us when we least expected it, blowing us and everything around us completely apart! As a family, we imploded and never recovered. The story of this particular night is a sad one and made sadder by the fact that it was my brother, the youngest and most defenseless member of the family, who ultimately paid the price. I never really forgave my parents for that.

When the following December event happened, I was eleven, and my brother was five. My brother was very excited, because he was finally going to start school the upcoming January. My mother had just purchased him new clothes for school, and we were all looking forward to Christmas.

On the weekends, my brother and I were subjected to my parents' friends, who were all heavy drinkers and party people. This particular Sunday we were to visit a couple whom we regularly visited. The man was the manager of a large, international wool auction factory in an industrial area. He lived in an apartment on-site with his wife. Both were alcoholics, especially the wife who, I remember, was often drunk in bed and unable to even participate in the visit. I liked to visit them at the factory, because it had wooden floors and lots of big walls. I could take my tennis racket and tennis balls with me and spend the time hitting the balls against the walls. It saved both me and my brother from being forced to watch four people getting drunker and drunker.

We were let into the factory by both the manager and my father. We would switch the lights on, and they would leave us alone there until my parents were ready to leave, which was usually late at night. By the time my brother was five, he was also starting to play tennis. This particular night we hit the ball back and forth together for quite some time before adventuring in the factory as we always did after playing tennis.

The factory was very large and very long. Raw wool of different grades lay in piles on the wooden factory floors where buyers from all over the world would view the wool and buy it during auction. During the weekends, there was no activity, and everything was closed down. Once the wool was purchased, it was bundled into one hundred-pound bales and placed on a slow-moving conveyor belt, which took it to different areas of the factory to be deposited onto transport trains underneath the factory floor. The bales were deposited onto the transport trains through one of the many large square cutouts in the factory floor. This was our playground.

As time went on, we got more and more adventurous and began to play on the conveyor belts. It was close to the floor and was made up of slats of wood about one foot apart. In its entirety, it was a series of conveyor belts joined together by steel rollers where one belt ended and another joined. The conveyor belts ran the entire length of the factory. Every individual conveyor belt was independently controlled by a little electrical box, which allowed it to be switched on or off. This was perfect for us. I would put my brother on the belt and start it up at the first switch box. As he moved slowly forward, I would run to the belt several slats behind him and jump on while it was moving. Then it was my brother's job to press the stop button at the second switch box before the conveyor belt reached the steel rollers and looped underneath. When it was stopped, I would then jump off, help my brother off, and then we would run to the beginning of the belt again and repeat this over and over until we tired of the game.

On this particular evening, we had first played tennis together, and then my brother had asked me to put him on a trolley and wheel him around the factory. It was a strange, eerie evening and very windy. The big trees outside of the factory scratched against the large glass windows. As I pushed and wheeled my brother around the edge of the factory, we chatted. I don't remember what we talked about, and I was completely unaware at that time, of course, that these were the last words we would ever say to each other. I did reflect back on it later, though, and it seemed that my brother had wanted to spend these last moments of his life together with me, enjoying quality time. I will always have these precious moments and was so grateful for them later. It was our last good-bye without us knowing. We were together and bonded as younger brother and older sister—us against the world in our own little created space of love and play.

And then we were ready for our conveyor belt ride. This time, however, I decided to push our adventuring a little further. When I placed my brother on the wooden slat of the belt, I gave him instructions to not stop the belt at the end as usual but to go onto the steel rollers and wait for me there. He was already moving forward on the belt when I jumped on at the beginning. As he reached the end, he turned around toward me and with the index finger of his left hand hovering right above the button, he asked, "Should I stop it?"

It seemed very important at the time not to stop the belt. I will never know why. But I replied with a strong, "No! Put your legs up, go onto the rollers, and wait for me." As he attempted to raise his legs to scoot onto the rollers, which was impossible in retrospect, he slipped backward. His little bottom fell between the front and back slats, and as the front slat slipped under the steel rollers, he was caught in between the wooden slat at his back and the steel rollers. While his legs were pushed tightly against his chest, he was slowly crushed to death by the power of the running machinery.

By the time I realized what was happening and jumped off to help him, he was wedged in too tightly. I could not pull him out despite my best frantic efforts. The electrical box had a reverse button, but it did not work. When I pressed reverse, the belt moved forward instead, wedging him in even tighter. At this point, I was screaming with frustration and hysteria and ran for my father to help me release my brother. As I burst into the apartment, the four adults were so drunk that all I got were dull looks as I screamed hysterically for somebody to help me. In desperation, because they seemed to be reacting so slowly, I pulled my father's hand and told him to follow me instead of trying to explain the terrible situation.

Everything is a blur after that. I do know my father managed to break the wooden slat at my brother's back to release him. In their panic, my mother and father rushed my brother to the nearest hospital and left me behind with the two drunks. I was extremely distraught and traumatized and needed somebody to comfort me so badly. These two drunks were in no position to do so. I did the only thing I knew to escape the horrible reality. Lying in the fetal position on the couch, I sunk into a deep, dark, depressive hole and fell mercifully asleep. And in my grief, I have never felt so alone.

It was very late when my parents finally arrived back to fetch me. My brother was no longer with them. He was gone. We rode home in silence—a demolished family. As we walked down the long, steep pathway toward our house, now just three of us, I remember my mother saying, "Let's hope this is just a nightmare, and when we wake up tomorrow, everything will be the same as it was before." Of course, it wasn't. The fragile fabric of our family was torn to shreds, impossible to repair.

Security is mostly superstition. It does not exist in nature, nor do the children of men as a whole experience it. Avoiding danger is no safer in the long run than outright exposure. Life is either a daring adventure, or nothing. To keep our faces toward change and behave like free spirits in the presence of fate is strength undefeatable!

—Helen Keller, 1957

TWO

My Life Eleven to Twenty-Three Years Old

With shock trauma, there is such a shattering of the heart, such an emotional explosion, that even at eleven years old, I looked around at my inner self and the millions of broken pieces and wondered in terror how I was ever going to mend myself. I felt an immediate desperation to do so—to make everything like it was before as quickly as possible. No matter how miserable, insecure, and joyless my life was prior to my brother's death, it was nothing in comparison to this. My parents had completely collapsed under the strain, shock, and guilt, and once again, they were of very little use to me.

I used all of my inner resources and called upon all the spiritual entities I was aware of at that young age to help me. The guidance, I believe, came quickly, together with my own survival instincts. My first step was the need to be among my peers, my school friends. The day after the tragedy, Monday morning, I chose to go back to school. I was being encouraged to stay at home, but I knew staying home would not help me. It was just too sad and too black and depressing experiencing all the sympathetic visitors and tears. I needed the beautiful, innocent child energy around me—playful and happy and without guilt, judgments, and depressive darkness. While shocked teachers kept trying to send me home, my immediate strength came from my friends who were on the same energetic level as myself, and I was very aware of this. They loved and supported me like children do, not dwelling on the tragedy but enfolding me into their therapeutic play world, which is exactly what I needed at that early and immediate point of recovery.

My second great resource was tennis. By this time, I was becoming very good at it, and I loved to compete against other athletes. This also took me away from reality. While on the court, I was very present in the moment—I had to be during the required focus and concentration. Therefore, I was far away from the awful thoughts, negative memories, and ugly pictures in my head.

I do remember crying many tears while trying to release the unbearable pain I felt. But when my parents held the funeral for my brother, I chose not to attend. They honored my decision. Instead, I went to represent my school in a tennis tournament that day. It seemed more positive. I was too furious with my parents at that point to want to attend with them. As far as I was concerned, my brother was gone due to lack of parental protection, neglect, and stupidity. Nothing was bringing him back, and I had a great compulsion to keep marching forward toward healing, as opposed to dwelling on an event we could do absolutely nothing to undo. Our lives changed dramatically after Matthew's death, but not much for the better that I could see.

My mother joined a church nearby and forced both me and my father to attend with her every Sunday. Initially, this seemed like a good thing. It helped with their guilt, I suppose. Attempts were made at giving up smoking and drinking, but unfortunately, this was more as a false facade for the benefit of new church friends. The crazy boozing, parties, and dysfunctional friends continued at all other times in our home. I later found out that the drinking was compounded with pain pills, at least in the case of my mother. If we were dysfunctional before, we were more so now.

We began to live in a weird, double-standard world. At church, my mother was all smiles and joy and good girl, but at home, she continued the constant and unrelenting yelling, screaming, nagging, and criticizing of her two remaining family members. Her actions at home destroyed anything that resembled warmth, love, and peace. It was also very confusing as a growing child to witness this hypocritical double personality switch back and forth at will. This also sickened my father, who expressed this often to me, because most of the abuse at home was directed toward him.

I began to really observe that my mother had a definite split personality. To the outside world she was all charm, warmth and kisses, and people experiencing this personality believed it and loved her. At home she could not be more cold, unlikable, and unloving toward both me and my father. While my father also realized and highly resented this, he did nothing to change it either. He was her enabler. For me it was just another reason not to trust them, and I found myself steadily divorcing myself from them both.

My Life Eleven to Twenty-Three Years Old

To survive this atmosphere, it was necessary to start emotionally numbing myself. I also decided that it seemed far safer to start relying on myself first and foremost. The alternative was to count on the fact that reliable thinking and decisions would be made by a couple who clearly did not like each other, who pulled in divided directions instead of together, and who lived each day creating household chaos, dysfunction, and anxiety. As a child, it was awful and extremely stressful living daily in this kind of ugly, insecure environment.

Another huge change in our family dynamic was that fear had set in with both my parents. I suppose it was a natural result of the terrible trauma, but I suddenly found myself at the center of all their attentions. They wanted to know everything about me. I couldn't even ride a bike, because they were so afraid I would hurt myself! Life went from one extreme to another. I was used to doing anything I wanted without anybody particularly caring, and suddenly I couldn't do anything without their approval. It was utterly suffocating to me. I felt so under the microscope that I started to look for escapes.

I began to notice changes in myself as well, especially on the tennis court. I seemed to react differently. I became very angry, very fast when things were not going my way. And I would become incredibly frustrated when I felt things weren't going perfectly. I became a control freak too. I tried so hard to get my power back, and I attempted this by becoming very controlling and achievement oriented. I felt good again only when I was winning competitions and prizes.

During trauma, one loses many things. The most devastating and immediate losses are the following: loss of power, expression, boundaries, sense of self, wild instinctual nature, and choice. Finally, hopelessness creeps in. In our attempt to heal ourselves, we try to find these things again. However, the onset of PTSD makes this almost impossible, because the brain is no longer working correctly. So, as an alternative, we will alter our behaviors in order to find the necessary foundations and building blocks of the personality we possessed before.

I remember the feeling that I had changed, but I didn't know how to change back again. It just didn't reverse by itself. It seemed stuck in there and definitely got worse over time instead of getting better. When people tell you that traumatic memory dissipates with time, know that it does not apply to PTSD. This insidious disorder gets decidedly worse over time.

Later in the book, I will explain why. But at this time in my life, of course, I understood none of these things and just reacted and helplessly observed my negative changes.

With the unsound kind of decision-making that existed in my family, none of us attended counseling as we should have. I don't think my parents even considered that I may require it. They certainly never mentioned it to me. So we all went untreated, while the trauma settled further and further into our somas. While my mother and father further locked horns with each other in a chronically unhealthy husband-and-wife relationship, I started to attract the attentions of the young male species and found I liked the attention. With them, I found the affections I missed at home. With somebody special, I found the kind of love, closeness, warmth, happiness, and intimacy that was missing from my life. Sexuality came easily for me and started young. I craved such intimate connection. Because I was an attractive young teenager, I had no shortage of admirers either. So this became an easy resource for me to feel better and happier about myself.

As my tennis improved, I was entered into more and more adult competitions to push my game ahead faster. By the time I was thirteen, I was traveling to tournaments farther from home. At fourteen, I was playing at the international level and was often sent by plane to other cities with spending money and a return plane ticket. I began to love the independence and time away from home. While I always had a host family taking care of me and providing me housing, I had to watch my spending money carefully for the duration of my stay and had to fend for myself against those a great deal older than myself socially and in competition. This taught me great self-sufficiency and independence.

By this time, my mother had gone back to work, so during high school, I came back to an empty house. Since my brother's accident, I found I hated to be alone. It would make me feel so desperate, and I didn't understand why. I could not get over this feeling of impending doom when utterly alone. It was during this time that I became very rebellious at home and found my first real boyfriend. He filled this gaping hole of need enormously for me. He also played tennis, so we began to meet and practice together after my school day and his work day (he was twenty-one years old and had a car).

Soon, I slipped into my first intimate, sexual experience with him when I was fourteen. He waited until I was sixteen before we had intercourse

My Life Eleven to Twenty-Three Years Old

(the legal age in South Africa), but till then, our contact had involved lots of heavy petting. He was distracting me from tennis as well. I often preferred having sex with him to playing tennis. I don't know what my parents thought was going on really, and I didn't care, but neither one pulled me aside to assess the relationship and make sure I was 'safe'. By the time they suspected I was sexually active, my boyfriend and I were well experienced with each other. I was so willful and rebellious at that point that there wasn't much they could do to stop it. We spent a year having unprotected sex before breaking up, and almost immediately, I started a relationship with the handsome boy down the road. He was four years older than me, and I had been fantasizing about him for years. I was seventeen.

In order to see him during the week (since we didn't have a tennis connection), he pretended to give me lessons in science. Lessons didn't last long in the evenings, and after my parents had gone to bed, science quickly turned into sex lessons right there in the living room—again, unprotected. Sex was the only thing that made me feel really good, and we soon progressed into very regular sessions whenever we could. I was doing terrible at school, and I didn't really care. Tennis had also become very demanding of me. Between tournaments, weekend leagues, daily tennis training, my active sex life, and weekend partying, schoolwork was the last thing on my mind. I was now one of the top players in my country, which definitely compensated for my lack of empowerment. Plus, I was madly involved and in love with the boy of my dreams, which fed me plenty of dopamine, making me feel good and happy.

But in my academically demanding final year of high school, things began to crash in on me on many fronts. Reality set in, and I was becoming overwhelmed with the need to perform at very high levels on the tennis court, pass my final year of high school exams, and keep a very demanding boyfriend happy and content, all while enduring the rigors of our continually miserable home life. Since my brother's death, I had also developed asthma and allergies (which remained largely untreated). During periods of stress, I would break out in hives and swelling and sometimes couldn't breathe at night. Something had to go. I had to pass my last year of high school. I couldn't even imagine failing and spending any more time at school. So I was particularly stressed during this period of time and developed an extremely painful condition called spastic colitis.

In reality, my life was spinning out of control. My focus was in all the wrong directions. I started drinking alcohol whenever my boyfriend and I went out. My studies were way, way behind where they should have been to pass. I had the South African Junior Championships looming, which I was expected to win. I was having lots of distractions from the boyfriend, who was very jealous of the attention that being a tennis star brought. He hated my tennis, and as a result, my parents began to interfere in our relationship. The problem was that at this point in my life, I really hated my parents and wanted as little to do with them as possible. The more they interfered with my life, the more rebellious and detached I became. I was uncontrollable.

By this time, my rage knew no bounds. It was never wise to provoke that part of me, which my mother did often. I began to see fear in her eyes when I lashed back at her with hatred after she'd start in on me. Even then, there continued to be no real guidance or solutions from either of my parents. As parents, they were totally ineffectual. Although I was trying very hard to guide my own life, I wasn't doing a very good job. As the walls closed in on me, it felt very claustrophobic indeed. I felt this growing, desperate need to be free of it all!

The South African Junior Championship was a disaster for me. My longtime coach was dying of cancer and could not support me when I needed it most. Getting any real support from my family was never anything I could count on. I was way behind on my studies at school, which weighed heavily on my mind while I attempted to win the championship. In the end, I disappointed myself beyond belief when I lost in the finals to a younger opponent and fellow teammate who was not better than me but not as mentally shaky as I was at that moment. It was a very bitter pill to swallow. In the space of a month, I lost my coach, lost the championship I really wanted and was expected to win, and seemed to be on the path to sure failure in my final high school year. To say I was stressed—an environment a trauma survivor does not thrive in—would be an understatement!

There were some silver linings that particular year, however. I went on to win a Provincial Senior Women's Singles title, and then I temporarily gave up tennis to study for several months. I managed (I don't know how) to pass my matriculation exams. I was free of school at last! But I had nothing to go to. I felt lost. My parents had made it clear there was no money for studying. Tennis with all its unfair politics and stresses was not something that I thought I really wanted anymore. No thought or guidance had been given by my parents on what I should be doing after high school. There was no next step, so I stepped into an empty abyss.

At this time, my boyfriend became my closest friend. We shared everything together. He became my family and my physical and emotional rock. After high school, I spent a year piddling around at some jobs before deciding that I had to get something more solid going. He suggested nursing. Two of his three sisters had studied nursing, and it sounded like a plan I could do. I could study at a teaching hospital, which would pay for my four years of training, as well as my room and board. The arrangement would also give me the freedom to move out of my parents' house at last.

The hospital accepted my application, and I was able to move into the student nursing quarters with a small salary. Finally, I felt as if I belonged to something structured and solid. I was happily independent of the stresses in my parents' home. My new circle of friends was made up of doctors and nurses. I was eighteen years old.

I did well at nursing. I had a natural empathy for patients and apparently had the respect of other student nurses when they voted me head student nurse of my group. The nursing program required that I study three months in the college adjoining the hospital. For the following three months, I was to perform nursing duties, alternating back and forth between college, passing the required exams, then three months working on a particular assigned ward, and then passing practical exams on work performed there. When we were off duty, we had to follow the strict rules of the student nurse hostel. We had to sign out and return well before midnight in order to sign in again before the doors were shut for the night.

This is where we ran into trouble. My boyfriend and I were used to dating whenever we wanted, often staying out well past midnight. He didn't like the new schedule, which definitely restricted his contact with me, and I soon noticed he was seeing less and less of me. On an emotional level, this was very destructive for me, because I relied so much on him for this vital need. Coping with sick people during the day and then not seeing him much at night was painful and lonely. When I discovered that while continuing to date me he was dating another girl within our close circle of friends behind my back, I was devastated and hurt beyond words! I was, of course, being emotionally manipulated by him and punished for not being available, but I was only to learn of these things later on. By the end of my first nursing year, I gave up nursing to try and get my relationship with him back on track. At the time, the relationship seemed more important, and so disappeared my opportunity at a good career. I returned home to my parents once again.

I was attempting to put my relationship back together with him, but I had lost trust in him and confidence in myself. When you are so young and counting entirely on one person for your emotional needs, they erroneously become your whole world. When they let you down, cheat on you, and hurt you, it is also very destructive to your self-worth and self-confidence. I started to buckle and become unsure of myself and more desperate to please him.

He took advantage of my strong emotional needs and used them to dominate me and bend me to his will. I was never sure if he was pleased with me or if he was cheating behind my back. As a result, I became even more subservient to do anything he wanted in order to get his attentions and affections. I was careful not to anger him and always tried to be in his good graces. This became the focus of my life. It seemed the more unsure I was of his affections for me, the more he seemed to enjoy it. He used my uncertainty to do whatever he desired with me and control me. My entire world began to revolve around pleasing him and getting him to love me instead of what it should have been at that age—looking to get myself on my own two feet and qualified for a future career so I could support myself. That was something he did not seem to want to encourage at all at this point.

It was during this period that I met another young man who was to be very influential in my life. He was a very handsome, very talented professional tennis player who traveled the world playing on the tennis circuits. I had met him one weekend at my tennis club during one of my many breakup periods with my boyfriend. The attraction between us was powerful and immediate. With him, I got my second chance at getting my life on some kind of solid track. He encouraged me to start playing tennis again and practiced many hours with me to get me back in shape. Of course, with this new budding romance, the now ex-boyfriend, who had heard about the romance, was trying his best to get me back.

The new boyfriend, David, was in South Africa for a short time visiting his family before he was scheduled to return to England and France for the tennis tournaments in the summer months. He proposed that I join him on the tour in France to play in the French Open Championships and then in

England to try to qualify for Wimbledon by playing in several pre-Wimbledon tournaments. He offered to travel with me, partner with me in mixed doubles, and practice with me to get my game up to top international standards so I could compete with the best tennis players in the world. I agreed.

The more time I spent with David, the more the ex-boyfriend, Chris, wanted to make up with me. Eventually, I was seeing both, and life became complicated again. By the time I left for Europe, David was hurt because of my continuing relationship with Chris. At the same time, Chris hated David. I couldn't choose which one I preferred.

My tennis suffered, as did my roller coaster of emotions. While traveling overseas with David, I received letters almost every day from Chris. He begged me to come back to South Africa and told me how much he loved me. As a result, I kept David at emotional arm's length, which started to affect our relationship. By the time we ended our tour of France and England, David asked me to continue to America with him. I refused.

I had also caught a terrible cold, which had turned into a very nasty chest infection. I felt ill and conflicted, wanting only to return to the familiar. Arriving back in South Africa, I was met at the airport by Chris, who was carrying flowers and a diamond engagement ring. And so, unbeknownst to me and like a lamb to the slaughter, began the darkest period of my life. Little did I know at the time that future events with him would disrupt and destroy life as I knew it so completely that I would find myself running for my life to the other side of the world in search of safety and protection. For the moment though, I was mercifully and blissfully oblivious to my sealed and fated future. I blindly surrendered into his handsome arms—into a magical world of African travel adventures, beach parties, fun nights out, candlelight dinners in the glittering town, and, of course, delicious, intense sex. I had just turned nineteen.

When one has experienced trauma from family dysfunction and abuse from a very young age, it is all you know. How can you know anything else? How would you know what a healthy life looks and feels like? Of course, at the time, I didn't realize or understand the enormous impact that all the family dysfunction one experiences in childhood has on life. It causes one to begin to repeat the trauma cycle by repeating the same dysfunctional behaviors you have learned from your family environment. I was no different. I had learnt my lessons well and, unfortunately, had absorbed the chaotic atmosphere like a little sponge. Because all this dysfunction and chaos was associated with love in my mind, I found myself repeating this cycle over and over.

Bearing this in mind, the stability of the engagement didn't last long. Our pattern of intense fighting, breaking up, and making up, and all the intense sex that followed, became our regular *modus operandi*. It was a constant wild ride of emotional ups and downs. We sought it out. When things went too well, we created drama to destroy it and start again. It was very stressful, but stress in one form or another was comfortable to me. In some sick, twisted way I needed it, and so did he.

It is another fact that like attracts like. It is common that two people from traumatic family backgrounds would be attracted to each other and repeat the negative family behaviors. It is such a familiar, learned response that it's tolerated by both parties. Of course, our parents recognized that our relationship was not going in any positive direction and tried their best to discourage it. The more they tried, the more we pulled together. It was us against the world—a concept I understood well. But it was when his parents sent him overseas for a year that our relationship kicked up to a new level of darkness.

By then, my tennis had been abandoned. Chris hated the attention it brought me. He hated the short dresses and the fact that men looked at my legs, he said. I wanted to please him, so I gave it up. Without this valuable, strengthening emotional resource, I found myself been drawn into his vortex where he was everything to me. So when his parents decided he needed a year overseas away from me, it was with great determination that we, in secret, planned for me to join him. I sold every prize I had ever won at tennis (which was quite a collection) to pay for the airfare and spending money. He was already in Europe for a couple of months when I flew to join him. I was met by Chris and two other friends, a male and female, in a van that had been bought in Holland and was equipped for camping. So off we went on our exciting European adventure.

It was almost immediately that I found myself pregnant. I was in love, and I remember how wonderful the pregnancy felt. I wanted so badly for us to get married and have the baby together. My happiness was short-lived, however, when he decided that we absolutely could not get married or have the baby. He did not want it. I said I could not return home single and pregnant. Suddenly, the pregnancy became a huge stress and dilemma that was ruining the trip. When we should have been enjoying ourselves with abandon, we found ourselves trying to figure out what to do about our complicated situation. I was emotionally distraught and torn, and physically, I was experiencing intense morning sickness. I felt a great deal sicker when Chris told me that his brother-in-law was sending him money to pay for an abortion.

With no support, I felt I had no choice. So with the money sent to us, we set out for England where we would stay with some friends for the winter, find some work to support ourselves, and abort the pregnancy, which was quickly approaching the three-month mark. On arrival, we quickly found a doctor willing to perform the abortion and scheduled the date. We had both found work already, and it was in between our work schedules that we headed for the clinic and tragically annihilated our child.

The abortion had a terrible effect on me. I was very triggered with the events, which churned up strong emotional memories of my brother's death all over again. I got very ill with influenza, which infected my chest, so my breathing was restricted and congested. It was exactly how I was feeling on the emotional and mental levels. The open and blind trust I had in my boyfriend slammed shut.

What infuriated me was that we had discussed birth control in the past. He never wanted me on anything and always assured me that if I should ever become pregnant, we would marry so I wasn't to worry. I trusted him. Yet, when that day arrived, he balked completely. I discovered that I could no longer trust what he said. This was devastating to me, and I was furious! He was my sole source of emotional warmth and closeness, so with this destruction of trust, I felt truly lost. To make matters worse, I became aware once again that he had started seeing somebody else from work while we were living together overseas. His cheating during our entire relationship was repetitive, but after the abortion, I felt fragile and needed him more than ever before. To become aware of yet another dalliance at such a time in our relationship was more than I could bear, so I left him and headed back home to South Africa. It had turned out to be a disastrous period of time, and I returned home deeply hurt, lonely, empty, very depressed, and back to Mom and Dad.

It took a little while to find work again, and when I did, a guy friend told me about some small apartments near the beachfront that were available for a very low rent. He had lived there a long time and put in a good word for me with the management. Soon, for the first time, I moved into my own apartment. My guy friend was a very handsome karate expert and model, and we soon began to spend more and more time together. Initially, I wasn't in love with him, but I found him to be kind and considerate. When it crossed the line of friendship to relationship, I wrote to my boyfriend overseas and told him that I had met somebody and wanted to completely end our relationship. Almost immediately, I received a very short telegram telling me he was returning home!

In retrospect, I had so many opportunities to end my relationship with Chris. So why couldn't I? I believe that due to the lack of love and emotional warmth I experienced as a child, and which I believe is also a most powerful basic need of any human being, I sought it out with a lover. I found it with him, and he manipulated these feelings for his own selfish needs. It was a familiar dysfunctional relationship, and he took me jealously into his world, isolating me from friends and family but providing me with the emotional closeness I craved above all else. I did not feel strong on my own anymore. He had become my world. Like an addiction to a strong narcotic, I could not leave it for long. This time was no exception. He arrived back in South Africa and immediately moved into the small apartment with me, which naturally broke up the relationship I had going with the handsome model. He then pushed me for a marriage date. Sadly and incredibly, in my lack of empowerment, which he took full advantage of, I agreed.

We planned to marry that November. I should have been excited, but I discovered I was very, very angry with him. I severely underestimated the effects of the abortion on myself and our relationship. When we were intimate, this anger would emerge. I wanted to scratch his back with my nails to get him off of me. I was confused by these reactions, and over time, it was not dissipating but getting stronger. Previously, I had always experienced a highly satisfying sexual relationship with him, but I now found myself not wanting him to touch me at all! I did not know who to discuss this with, and it concerned me enormously because we were supposed to get married in a few months. So I went, in secret, to a psychotherapist for help. This psychotherapist sealed my fate. After a few long sessions with him, he suggested that I go ahead with the marriage. He went on to suggest that once married, I should get pregnant right away. The new child, he explained, would replace the one I had lost and would then dissipate the anger and angst I was feeling regarding my boyfriend and the abortion.

As the wedding date approached, however, I began to feel nauseated. I had the greatest desire to run away as fast as I possibly could. I worked with an older English woman who was always very helpful and kind to me, so I sought her advice. One night, about a week away from the wedding day, I told her how apprehensive I was feeling—a feeling of utter dread. As she explained it to me, all future brides feel nervous before their wedding days. In her opinion, my feelings were all quite normal. There was nothing to worry about, she said, and encouraged me to go ahead and enjoy the wedding. In my inexperience, what did I know? What could have prepared me for what was to come? Nothing, I think. It was beyond my personal understanding at the time.

And so the wedding day approached. The reception was booked at a beautiful downtown hotel where we expected about a hundred of our friends and family. The wedding itself went without a hitch. We spent our first night together as husband and wife in a honeymoon suite at the top of the hotel, and we had then planned a ten-day stay at Kruger National Park for our honeymoon. I felt tense and stressed and did not want him to touch me. The more he wanted to make love to me, the sicker I felt. Eventually, though, I relaxed enough to participate, but the angry feelings remained.

Sometime during the next month's December holidays, I found myself pregnant again much to everybody's delight. During the months of my pregnancy, we lived in a one-bedroom apartment and were relatively happy. As the birth date approached, my now-husband was scheduled to report for mandatory army duty for three months. He would, however, be with me for the birth. It was decided that once the baby arrived, the baby and I would go and live with his parents until his return when we would look for our own place.

I gave birth to a very pretty, healthy little girl, and I immediately went into a deep depression. My husband was about to leave us for three months, and I was living with my in-laws, whom I loved very much, but it wasn't the same as having my own space. My daughter was colicky right from the beginning and literally cried day and night. As a result, nobody was getting any sleep. My husband, who stayed with me for a week before taking off for military duty, wanted sex at every opportunity. I'd had a natural birth, but with an episiotomy, I was still obviously very tender and sore. He didn't seem to care much about that; he only cared about satisfying his own needs before he left. I quickly began to see how extraordinarily selfish he was. Besides the pain I was experiencing during intercourse, I also did not want to get pregnant. Once again, he did not want me on any birth control.

Living alone with my in-laws was difficult. They were an enormous help to both my daughter and I, but her constant crying made me feel very awkward, because they were also being deprived of sleep. I felt very depressed and exhausted and could not shake it off. By the time my husband arrived home, I couldn't wait for us to find our own place together. We ended up in a two-bedroom apartment in a nice neighborhood and settled down to make a home for our young family. I was happy to have him back.

I am not sure of the exact moment when the physical abuse started. In reality, it started way back in our relationship, but it was so gradual and so subtle that I hadn't noticed right away. I do remember one evening overseas when we were alone and I had suspected that he was seeing another girl at work. I had confronted him about it as we were sitting in the kitchen eating dinner. He slapped me across the face very hard for questioning him. I remember being absolutely stunned. But since that day, he had not touched me that way again. But true to our *modus operandi*, peacefulness and security would not last long before we created the usual drama and instability.

He started off insulting me and calling me stupid on a daily basis. He was still insistent that I not play tennis, because he said that men looked at my legs when I wore the short tennis dresses, which drove him crazy with jealousy. Although I longed to get onto the tennis court again, on the rare occasions I did, it caused such domestic strife that it just wasn't worth it. He no longer wanted me to work and did not encourage contact with my parents or invite our friends over. I was becoming more and more isolated.

He very quickly had a routine set out for me. We would wake up and have sex. Then, while he showered for work, I was expected to cook breakfast. During the day, of course, I took care of my daughter. When he returned home at night, he expected dinner and sex again before going to sleep. During weekends, he wanted sex three times a day and sometimes more. It was excessive. He introduced me to pornographic books to look at and read, but I finally drew the line one day when he told me he was bringing home a photographer friend of his to take nude photos of me. My refusal to comply with this demand displeased him very much.

The constant crying of the baby made domestic life very difficult and even more stressful. I was not sleeping much at all, but I tried to rest with her during the day when she finally fell into an exhausted sleep. I began losing weight. As our marriage progressed, it was becoming more and more abusive. True to his nature, when things got tough, he simply went out and came back very late at night. When I would question where he had been while I was left alone with the crying baby night after night, he started hitting me, grabbing my clothes, throwing me around the room, and insulting me. The more this behavior escalated, the more I did not want to have sex with him, which only served to infuriate him more. When I rejected his requests and expectation of sex, he would go into a tirade, wait for me to fall asleep, and then attack me sexually, attempting penetration.

The fighting and yelling and physical, mental, and emotional abuse were now escalating at a frightening pace. I remember screaming in fear night after night during his physical attacks. Although I am sure the neighbors could hear this, everybody just turned a blind eye and went on as if nothing was wrong. He was much stronger than me, so I was starting to worry about my well-being and that of my daughter. He would now erupt at the least thing—when she cried at night or when I had to ask for more money to buy food. I barely had any clothes, because he bought me none, and because I no longer worked and didn't have my own money, I could not buy any for myself. I had bruises all over my body, and the screaming and yelling episodes were now very frequent. During the day when I would take my daughter to the beach, he began to question what I was doing during the day and demanded I give him a full accounting of my whereabouts. Soon he was accusing me of seeing other men during the day, which gave him an excuse to punish me because I had caused the situation, he said. The abuse was escalating, and he now demanded full compliance from me for all his demands. At this point, my self-confidence was almost completely destroyed. According to him, everything was my fault, which was what caused him to punish me to keep me in control.

I felt beaten down and depressed with the marriage. I knew that I never wanted to have another baby with him, and I knew that in order to survive, I had to get out. Of this, I was sure. So, I secretly started to take matters into my own hands. He was constantly telling me he wanted a son and was actively trying to get me pregnant. I felt my chances of escape from this marriage would be severely limited once I had another child, so I could not let that happen. I approached my gynecologist and explained my situation. He said he would insert an IUD (birth control device) during the guise of a uterine scrape that he told my husband I needed. And so I protected myself from his sexual attacks.

I was determined to leave the marriage at this point but was carefully waiting for the best opportunity. I had previously tried to leave one night. In order to stop me, he dragged me kicking and screaming by my long hair from the front door to the living room where he threw me across the room. He then hit me and warned me never to try that again. Despite this, however, an accelerated incentive came after one truly awful night when I began to seriously fear for my life and the safety of my daughter. We had by now been married for two years.

After I had put my daughter to bed, we went to bed. As usual, he demanded sex, and I refused him. I felt nauseated and didn't even remotely want to be intimate with him anymore. He was furious with me and, as usual, started yelling at me and insulting me. At this point, my daughter woke up crying. He jumped up, screaming that she should shut up and then rushed into her bedroom. I had never seen him attack our daughter before that night. I rushed into the baby's room on his heels to protect her.

I got into the room just as he lifted her up in her crib and slammed her down hard onto the mattress. She was still screaming. I was infuriated! It was the first time I had witnessed him hurt her. Tolerating him hurting me was one thing, but seeing him hurt her brought out all my rage and protective instincts. Before he could pick her up again, I had raked my long nails down his back to distract his focus from her to me. I realized the moment I did this that all his anger would now be turned on me. It only took one look from him for me to realize that I should run for the front door as fast as I could to escape. I didn't reach the door before he pulled me back by my hair and dragged me into the living room where he proceeded to bang my head repeatedly into the sharp edge of the wooden window sill.

I could tell by his glazed eyes that he had dissociated. As he was smashing my head into the sharp-edged shelf, I thought for the first time that it was possible that I may be seriously hurt or killed. I started yelling his name to bring some focus to his eyes. As he came out of his glazed state and started to focus on my face, he stopped. Then came the usual apologies. But for me, the damage was done. I was finally really finished with this and was determined and very focused on how to leave as soon as possible. I also realized I would have to be very careful how I made my exit, because I knew he would never allow me to leave.

A friend recently told me that some men don't take wives; they take prisoners. This is precisely how I felt. During the worst, darkest period of this negative experience, in desperation, I went to see a psychiatrist. I felt very depressed and beaten down. During one of the sessions, he gave me a truth serum to try to find out what my underlying issues were. I remember that all I could do was cry out hysterically that I wanted to be free! It made things very clear for me, and I knew I had to find the strength and opportunity to leave my husband. That's easier said than done when you are reduced to such emotional weakness. Adding to this, the choice was not easy. Society, back then, frowned on divorcing or leaving your husband, no matter what the reasons. To complicate things more, I had a child. As the saying goes, "You made your bed; now you must lie in it."

By my husband's deliberate design and my lack of empowerment, I was not well educated and had not worked in two years. With a child, this was not a secure situation by any means. We had a little money in a savings account, but not much. I felt neither my parents nor his would understand, so it was a terrible dilemma on what to do and how to extricate myself from my horrible marriage. For the first time, I began to think of suicide. This was shocking to me. When I walked down the aisle, I never thought in a million years that the marriage would break down. It just never occurred to me that my predicament was a possibility. To defend myself and survive, I simply numbed out and just took everything he was dishing out to me until he could not reach me or hurt me emotionally anymore. Within my two-year marriage, I had become a very depressed, very unhappy, and very thin walking domestic abuse zombie.

There were the many thoughts going through my head after the episode when he attacked my daughter. I saw that this was a new escalation of violence and fear to emotionally hurt me. This event, luckily, snapped me out of my numbed state, and all of my natural protective mother instincts kicked in. Now I suddenly found myself highly motivated to gain freedom for the both of us. My basic animal instincts also told me that I had to be very cautious and make my moves very carefully and vigilantly without him knowing in advance. If not, there would be serious physical consequences for me and my daughter.

I believe now that I was in the hands of a dangerous psychopath. Unfortunately, because of my upbringing with a psychopathic mother, this was familiar to me. Today, I thank God that I was able to find a brief moment of strength to leave him. Over the years, I have read of so many women who just could not find the strength to leave their awful circumstances. Instead, they continued, in legitimate fear, to stay with these sick men for years and years, experiencing escalating violence and abuse. All the while, their children watched these repetitive events in horror, often becoming direct victims themselves and becoming traumatized in the cycle of domestic abuse.

I feel that if I had been emotionally healthy, I would have left him when I received that first hard slap in the face in the overseas flat (or maybe way before that). That is what a healthy woman in possession of confidence and healthy boundaries would do. But at that time, I had none of those things. Rather, I was so insecure, starved, and needy for any kind of love and affection that I was willing to subject myself to him under all circumstances in order to get from him what I should have received as a child. In his need to control others to make himself feel strong, I became the perfect, willing victim. I had been carefully groomed and slowly trained over the years to obey, please, and suffer his angry abuse and punishments when I did not comply. Complicity was rewarded with his approval, love, and affection.

I waited a few days. True to all domestic abuse situations, his apologies and remorse would always come on the heels of the abuse. Now, however, I knew better. His negative behaviors were getting worse quickly. The time in between episodes was becoming shorter and the attacks more brutal. I knew it was just a matter of time before another event played out. I did not plan on being there when it did. So I took full advantage of this respite period when he was on his better behavior and waited for the best opportunity to make our escape.

It came on a sunny, bright morning after I had watched him drive off for work. The moment I saw his car turn the corner I sprang into action. Grabbing two suitcases, I filled them with all the personal belongings I could fit. I had a key to my mother and father's house and headed there in the car with my daughter. When I had situated us in the house, I called my mother, who was at work at the time, and explained to her what was going on. This was one time, thank God, that she was supportive and said she would be home shortly. I was very afraid that when my husband found out where we were, he would come for us. I was right.

My parents were shocked to learn what had been going on during my marriage. Thankfully, they were protective. They told me to go into the bathroom and lock myself in. True to my husband's nature, he arrived in a fury that evening at the front door and demanded to see me. My parents would not allow him into the house. He tried to push through the front door, but they held him back and told him to leave me alone and go home.

My Life Eleven to Twenty-Three Years Old

So began six months of anxiety-ridden hell for me. I told my husband I wanted a divorce. He had his parents visit one night to demand that my parents send me back home to him. My parents refused. He stalked me, and I would often hear him walking around our house at night. As he realized over time that I would never be returning to him, he started to threaten me. He said I would never separate him from his daughter, and no matter where we went in the world, he would track us down and find us. It was during these threats that I seriously started to consider what to do with my daughter. Having already suffered abuse from him, I took these threats very seriously and did not want to even consider what would take place if he discovered us alone.

I found myself in another difficult decision-making situation—how to keep my daughter safe from her father. I came up with a very unorthodox solution. It was one I felt would work to free us both, although at great personal sacrifice. As I saw it, as long as my daughter and I were together, we would never be free of him and would always be looking over our shoulders in fear. It was a terrible, terrible dilemma, but the more he threatened, the more desperate I became to find a solution to the problem.

His oldest sister had five children and was longing for a sixth but was told she could have no more children. I met with her and explained that I would love it if she would take my daughter and raise her in her own family. She had a beautiful, stable home with a wonderful husband. She agreed. In the divorce papers, I said I would give up all rights to my daughter on the condition she was raised by my sister- and brother-in-law. All agreed.

Six months later, I was granted my divorce from him and watched him pick up my daughter to drive her to his sister's house. It was by far the most heart-wrenching experience I have ever felt or ever want to feel again. This was a new low in my life, and I vowed that it must end. From that point on, I had to get on with my life by starting to reverse the awful, destructive cycle of behavior and choices I had been making that were ruining my life and making it miserable and unbearable. I was twenty-three years old, but I was now finally free of him!

It is my hope that anybody, man or woman, in a similar situation would leave this dangerous environment immediately. These situations do not improve but only escalate with time! Since the seventies, society is much more aware of the domestic abuse syndrome, and many shelters have opened to help people escape the abuse and get back on their feet. Go to the nearest police station or hospital and ask for help to find a nearby shelter. There are now also networks of compassionate people in place who can help secretly protect you if it becomes necessary to disappear from these very dangerous people who are hunting you down. The domestic abuse shelters will also know of this network and how to connect with them if needed. Ultimately, you are the only one who can alert others to your plight and make the move to leave in order to protect yourself and any children you may have in your care. Find some strength and courage. Find the opportunity and then flee. You will never, never regret you did this!

For those interested in learning more about how we can protect ourselves by recognizing a psychopath, there is a wonderfully informative web site at www.psychopathyawareness.wordpress.com. According to the latest statistics, anywhere from 1% to 4% of society are psychopaths. Not surprisingly, a high percentage of prison inmates meet the diagnostic criteria for psychopathy. It must be also be noted, however, that most psychopaths are not the Ted Bundy (sadistic psychopath) type, but never-the-less cause a great deal of chaos and suffering amongst us. If these statistics are true, then it is very likely we are meeting these often very charming people and bumping into them each and every day. This is a very scary thought! We would all be well advised to learn as much as we can about psychopaths, what attracts them and how to avoid being targeted by them, thereby protecting ourselves from the resulting misery they are capable of and enjoy creating in other peoples' lives!

THREE

Healing a Shattered Soul

In his book *Breakthrough*, Whitley Strieber, who writes interesting books about his direct contacts and conversations with aliens, has an epiphany on what the extraterrestrials have been trying to convey to him in their communications regarding guilt. He writes:

> *And then I saw it: this communication wasn't about getting forgiveness, it was like the journey to Eden, a lesson in the consequences of guilt.*
>
> *To be with the visitors/God, I had to be free. But freedom did not involve suppressing what I had done that was wrong. Pretending is a waste of time; the actions are engraved on the past.*
>
> *Like everybody, I'd sometimes wounded people in ways that were never going to heal. The message was clear: live with your sins, taste them, bear them, face what you have done and what you are. That is the direction of freedom.*

Likewise, in order to heal emotionally and be free of a traumatic past, there has to be brutal honesty with yourself—a facing of the dragon head-on. The hard, unforgiving pathway that leads from being a shattered soul to being whole, healthy, and thriving again is long and arduous but well worth the tremendous rigorous efforts it demands. It cannot take place if you remain inwardly frozen and stuck in fear and guilt. It cannot take place if it remains suppressed inside you, and it cannot take place if you stubbornly insist on burying your head in the sand and pretending all is well when you know deep inside it is not.

Healing from trauma requires large measures of brave, courageous fighting; a nonacceptance of your present mental state; an overwhelming need to gain back the health of your original soul blueprint; and some outrage that situations out of your control created this inner monster with which you battle each and every day. When one is more afraid of the possibility of staying sick than getting better, you are more easily able to jump off the cliff, take your chances, look for the healing opportunities, and adopt an attitude of, "What have I got to lose?" I found myself in that place. I had lost everything. When I viewed my life with clarity and honesty, it looked like a train wreck. I found myself at the bottom of the barrel, and the only alternative direction I saw, other than death, was up.

After much thought, staying depressingly at the bottom of the barrel was not an option for me. It was unacceptable. Luckily, my self-survival skills were such that like a drowning woman whose lungs were bursting for air, I headed upward with great determination for life-giving oxygen. When it really came down to it, I did not want to drown. When I looked at things very honestly, I also realized that in order to move upward, I had no option but to sever the shackles of my past that were so debilitating to my well-being. The *root cause* of *my* trauma was my family, who continued with their dysfunctions and interferences in everything I did. This had contributed immeasurably to my demise. In order for me to survive and recuperate, I had to free myself of them and cut the heavy chains that bound me to them by birth. This turned out to be a life-saving decision.

Leaving Port Elizabeth, South Africa

After much thought, I decided to leave Port Elizabeth, the city of my birth, and head north to the city of Johannesburg where I would work and start a new life. As lonely and scary as this was in the beginning, it truly started me on a road to recovery that also became the beginning of my life's great adventure. For starters, Johannesburg salaries were much better. While my mother had initially helped me get a job through the photography company she worked for, after a few months, I found myself working in another position as a waitress in a downtown Johannesburg hotel.

This was a demanding but very exciting job in a well-known restaurant where I met many international business people, especially from America. I had always had a desire to go to America. I had missed one chance to go there with my tennis friend when he returned to Miami for a coaching job he had lined up in-between playing on the international tennis circuit. Instead, I had returned to South Africa to my boyfriend and our disastrous marriage. So now I was able to play with the idea again. I was working very long hours but also making a lot more money than I ever had before, so between a good salary and tip money, I began to save some money with the idea of someday taking a trip to see the United States of America.

My roommate in Johannesburg was an Austrian girl I met working in the hotel. She was a European-trained waitress/chef who was trying to learn English while working in South Africa. Because I could speak neither Austrian nor German, we were the perfect combination. She was making much more progress living with me than trying to learn English from the little pocket dictionary she had when I first met her.

The long hours of work from ten o'clock in the morning until two o'clock in the afternoon and then again from six o'clock in the evening until midnight afforded me little time to dwell on my emotional woes. On a deep emotional level, my pain was excruciating, and I missed my daughter terribly. There was just this constant, deep pain. As a solution, I simply worked to exhaustion, slept, and returned the next day for the same routine. I think I became a workaholic, but at the time, it felt therapeutic. It was what I needed.

My roommate and I also lived a fast-paced life in-between our work. Often, after work, we would hit the nightclubs of Johannesburg. Sometimes we danced till the sun came up, slept for a few hours, and then headed back to work. Our days off were spent going someplace with friends, traveling to visit friends, or sunbathing. It was a very social time for me. This too was what I needed. I just did not allow myself any time to dwell on the depressing negatives, and I spent as much time as possible with positive, fun friends.

But one day in June 1976, my life took a sharp, unexpected turn. The infamous Soweto riots broke out in Johannesburg. Growing up in the apartheid system was, for me, a very strange experience. I had never liked the extreme government or being forced to learn Afrikaans (a dialect of Dutch and German) in school. So when thousands of young, black children rampaged that year in the township of Soweto, Johannesburg also expressing their extreme resentment against having to learn Afrikaans in school, which represented a very repressive government toward them, I could well understand their frustrations. But it was the response from the government that was so brutal and altogether shocking and unacceptable to me.

I remember hearing that little children, twelve and younger, were being shot and killed by the hundreds. One evening at work we were informed that we were being housed in the hotel that night, because they were afraid of any of us walking home to our downtown apartments. I could hear the parents and relatives of the killed children. The group had run thirty miles into the heart of Johannesburg, smashing store windows in their utter outrage, fury, and frustration. I remember sitting in a little room where we rested before and after work and thinking to myself that this was the end for me. How could I possibly, in good conscience, continue to support a government that did such things? My heart, still so raw from the loss of my own child, could take no more. I decided that night I would leave the country. No more going out and spending my money. Every penny from then on was going to be saved so I could one day sever myself from my miserable childhood and the country of my birth.

My sights were set on America. I had spent time in Europe and didn't feel it was a place I would like to live permanently. At the same time I was contemplating leaving, other friends I knew were also looking to leave the country. Australia was offering free ship passage and would also pay the expenses of moving your possessions. Somehow Australia didn't attract me the same way America did. I think I felt my destiny. I didn't know how I would manage it, because I didn't have any close friends or family there to help me. But somehow, I knew that if I got myself there, America could be my new home and the new start in life that I needed so badly.

So, the social gatherings were cut down while I saved and saved to leave as quickly as possible. My roommate noticed the change in my social habits and asked me one day why I wasn't going out as much as before. I told her my intentions. After a day or so, she approached me and said she had also always wanted to visit America and wondered if I would mind her joining me. I agreed and, in truth, was very happy to have a travel companion. It would not have stopped me to go alone, because I was very determined, but having her company was so much nicer.

As the months passed, I was concerned that we were not saving money quickly enough to leave any time soon. The airfare was very expensive to and from the USA, and so far, we were on track with saving our spending money for a few months but not our airfare. I did some thinking. There is a coastal city called Durban on the Indian Ocean, north of where I had grown up. In the sailing world, Durban is famous for its large harbor and its Royal Yacht Club. It is one of the few places in Africa where yachts that are sailing around the world can stop to replenish food, water, and supplies. There are also dry docks for yacht repairs. Because of this, yachts sailing to the United States from Africa would stop there before undertaking the rigorous and dangerous passage to Cape Town, which was the final stop before crossing the Atlantic Ocean to America. I had remembered this and asked my girlfriend if she would agree to us working as crew on one of these boats if I could find work positions for us. She agreed.

I took a weekend off from work and headed for Durban where I quickly secured work for both of us on a beautiful German-built, American-owned, fifty-three-foot ketch headed for California. It was scheduled to leave South Africa in January 1977 from the port city of Cape Town. It was a crazy idea. Neither of us had ever sailed, let alone over an ocean, but I wanted desperately to get out of South Africa and did not want to stay another year trying to save money for the airfare. It was a solution, at least, and the problem of money for transport to the United States was solved.

Although we would not receive a salary, we would have a place to stay, be given food to eat, and, most importantly, would be delivered to our intended destination quickly. The plan was that we would meet the boat in Cape Town in January. Working toward our adventure, we bought specially priced US Greyhound bus tickets for foreigners for three months, gave notice at our jobs, sold and gave away our worldly possessions, changed the money we had saved to traveler's checks, updated our passports, visited the dentist so we had no problems while we traveled, and, finally, boarded a plane for Cape Town to throw our fate to the wind.

The voyage was expected to last about two months before we reached the Caribbean Islands and another month while we traveled through the Islands to Miami, Florida. We got a taxi from the airport to the shipping port of Cape Town to meet the yacht crew waiting for us and immediately hit our first big snag. The captain suddenly said he was not expecting my girlfriend to be coming along and refused to take her on board. I was surprised and mortified! I had been writing letters to him for about two months and always made it clear that she and I were travel companions, so I could not understand what he was trying to do. I tried to reason with him, but he was adamant. I thought hard about our predicament. We had sold everything, and we had no jobs or place to stay. I was not leaving without her. What game was he playing? I needed to think quickly.

I asked if we could at least come aboard and have a drink and some dinner and talk about it. He agreed, and it quickly became apparent what he wanted—me. We were trapped, and he had done it very well indeed. In my naïveté, I hadn't thought about this occurrence at all. He made it clear that he wanted sex from me, or we were not coming aboard as crew. I made it very clear that if I gave him sex, not just me but my girlfriend must also be included in the crew to America. I was furious! In anger, I decided to give him a night he would never forget. I apparently did my job well, as we left Cape Town harbor early the following morning—the captain, three men, my girlfriend, and me. But I was now concerned about the upcoming trip. I did not intend to sleep with him the entire trip. This was going to be interesting!

America, Here I Come

I finally left my country of birth with nothing but a backpack containing two pairs of jeans, some T-shirts, a pair of tennis shoes, a bikini, a jacket, and a good Pentax camera. I also had a whole lot more of hard-fought-for wisdom. The last thing I saw as we sailed away was the majestic Table Mountain. I sat on the deck with mixed emotions and watched it till I could see it no more. Then, I turned my head forward to the future and a new life. It felt like the world was lifted from my shoulders. I was twenty-four years old.

The proactive move to separate myself from the mess that my life had become was very therapeutic for me. In sailing over the ocean, I entered a surrealistic, unfamiliar world compared to what I was used to. This enabled me to finally climb out of the old, familiar, patterned groove I had been in for so long. Because the old groove was such a negative one, this was a wonderful opportunity to experience things on my own terms without interference of some kind or another. I found this very liberating and empowering. Having emotional space around me was healing, and having lots of time to think allowed me to begin to process and sort out events in my life that had led me to that point in time. In essence, I gave myself the gift of freedom that I had craved and needed for so long to recover from my unhappy, traumatic past.

The yacht trip became predictably difficult with the captain, and I found I got very seasick. The captain drank each night and passed out. He wanted sex often until I finally said no after several days out at sea. He was naturally unhappy and started to punish me in all sorts of ways. Well, what was new? I had played this game before, so it became a chess game of wills and pitting mind against mind. But I was not the one drinking each day, so it wasn't much of a contest. He often threatened to throw my girlfriend, who protected me, overboard. He threatened to rape me almost daily, gave me toilets to clean and rotting cabbages to prepare, and tried to keep me as sleep deprived as possible. On the plus side, I was too happy to have my freedom and be sailing to my destination to be brought down by him.

We went through many scary storms, losing our mizzenmast in one and becoming a sloop. I prayed a lot, and when I was the most scared, I surrendered myself to God. I was absolutely amazed when one day, after six difficult weeks at sea, we sailed into the little harbor of Grenada in the South Grenadine Islands of the Caribbean. I was ecstatic! My friend and I decided we were not traveling with this captain any farther. We joined the crew of another captain, happily living and playing in the Caribbean islands for another two months before finally flying to Florida, USA.

The New Colossus

Not like the brazen giant of Greek fame,
With conquering limbs astride from land to land;
Here at our sea-washed, sunset gates shall stand
A mighty woman with a torch, whose flame
Is the imprisoned lightning, and her name
Mother of Exiles. From her beacon-hand
Glows world-wide welcome; her mild eyes command
The air-bridged harbor that twin cities frame.
"Keep ancient lands, your storied pomp!" cries she
With silent lips. "Give me your tired, your poor,
Your huddled masses yearning to breathe free,
The wretched refuse of your teeming shore.
Send these, the homeless, tempest-tossed to me,
I lift my lamp beside the golden door!"

—Emma Lazarus, 1883

The Incredible Journey

We arrived safely on the shores of America in April 1977. For the next three months, we traveled everywhere in the United States and Canada that our bus tickets allowed. It was wonderful! We experienced new towns and cities and made many new friends along the way. Many kind Americans had given me their business cards when they were visiting South Africa with promises to show me around their part of the world if I ever made it to the United States. Without exception, everybody we called when we reached their home town graciously gave us a wonderful tour of the area where they lived. I am probably one of the very few people who have ever toured the military school of West Point, Virginia, for example. I fell in love with America and its people and decided this definitely would be a place I could live. I wanted to spend more time in America.

My girlfriend did not feel quite the same way. By the end of our three-month trip, she made the decision to leave for Switzerland where her boyfriend was waiting impatiently for her. We sadly parted ways in the middle of New York City. After we hugged good-bye and she climbed into a taxi headed for Kennedy Airport, I boarded a Greyhound bus headed for Aspen, Colorado. I had exactly three days left on my bus ticket and a promise of work from a guy we had met while passing through there.

When I counted my money, I had just seventy-three dollars left. I was desperate! I had called my parents collect from New York on my birthday at the end of June, but my mother, still fuming because I'd left the country (and their control, I think), refused to even accept the charges. I was never able to speak with them. I renewed my vow that no matter how fearful or desperate, I would never return to my family. With so little money and no job or supportive family to lean on, I was scared. But I was also armed with a new determination not to return to South Africa. It was simply no longer an option for me. Besides, I intuitively still carried a vague, comforting feeling that somehow everything would work out.

Healing in Aspen, Colorado

I ended up living in Aspen for a precious year. My friend, true to his word, put me to work immediately. He also found me a place to stay with a friend of his in a beautiful condominium overlooking the mountains, which were covered with evergreen pine trees and glorious aspens. I had the privilege of living and breathing in one of the most beautiful places on earth. It would be an understatement to say how much healing took place for me there. I made enormous strides. After spending many months in one place, rather than traveling, I finally found myself. I was able to rest emotionally. I was self-supporting and alone, which allowed me time to read, walk, play tennis, learn to ski, meet new and interesting people, and most importantly, process the last few years of my life.

Time and a lot of space are essential for those wishing to heal from trauma. It is a slow, natural process that simply requires one to take time and be patient with oneself. The healing process cannot be hurried or forced.

One man in particular became extremely helpful to me. He was a customer in the restaurant where I was waitressing. He sat alone in my serving station that day—a slim, handsome blonde man in his thirties. Because I was his waitress and we were clearly drawn and attracted to each other, we chatted in-between him ordering and me serving him lunch. It turned out that he was a physician who worked for the government in Washington, DC. He was also setting up the first alternative medicine center there. He told me he was in Colorado for a weeklong conference on battered wife syndrome. After listening to the story of my brief, nightmarish marriage, he invited me to attend the conference with him when I had time off. I took advantage of his offer and attended the lectures with him when I was able.

There, for the first time, I learned all about the syndrome that surrounds violence in marriages—how it starts, how it escalates, why men do it, and why women tolerate it, especially over long periods of time. In 1977, this was a subject finally coming out of the closet, so physicians could recognize the signs when women would come in for medical treatment. For me, recognizing all the signs and symptoms of my own personal experience was very enlightening. It took loads of guilt off my shoulders, as men in these relationships always have a way of blaming the women for their violence. *Their* behavior is always blamed on the women. I understood so much from being able to attend these medical lectures!

At the same time, I was starting to have out-of-body experiences. At night I was consciously leaving my body and flying around the mountains of Colorado and then returning to my body before having to wake up in the morning. My return to my body was less than perfect, though, and I often felt disorientated and out of focus during the day. My new physician friend was able to help with this too, because his interest in spirituality and meditation was extensive. He patiently explained to me how to return to my body correctly and also introduced me to the philosophical and spiritually enlightening Richard Bach books. This was my first real contact with metaphysics. At the time, I really did not realize that this would later form the foundation for my introduction to a spiritual path that would change me for the better and dramatically alter my life.

For those people who go through traumatic events, there is a great need to understand why this happened to them. This is especially true if you are a victim of abuse and cruelty you don't think you deserved. Why did you have to endure this experience? Finding answers that satisfy you is essential in the healing process. One of the places to find the answers is by investigating your own spirituality. There are many places to look in your search for answers—churches, spiritual groups, spiritual book shops, and now the Internet, which has a wealth of information. Any one of these sources may lead you to something that may finally give you a satisfying answer to these questions.

After two weeks, my physician friend returned to Washington, DC, and we never saw each other again. During the next two years, we talked on the phone from time to time. He was always a great and gentle teacher and healer. When I tried to contact him a few years down the road through a friend of his, I heard he had died of cancer but only after he had realized his dream of opening the first alternative medicine clinic in the city. I felt that I was fortunate in my healing process to have had him drop into my life at such a difficult juncture to shed light on my traumatic past. Such people continue to emerge in your life, I believe, when you are sincere and determined in your quest to heal.

I felt the need to leave Aspen in the spring of 1978. For one thing, it was way too cold for somebody who had grown up in the tropics as I had. I needed my blue skies and warm sunshine year-round. I had two choices—Florida or California. At the time I had two friends, a German girl and a Norwegian girl. The German girl wanted to go to California to study stained glass. The Norwegian girl owned two hairdressing salons and wanted to take a break. Because they were both heading west together, I decided to join them. On a map, we selected the romantic and alluring sounding place called Laguna Beach, California. After a large send-off from our friends, we set off on our adventure together in the German girl's blue Mustang.

There was sadness in leaving Aspen. It had given me so much in the way of healing. It had given me the space I needed to decompress. It had given me a beautiful, settled place to live, make friends, and earn income. I had discovered revelations about my past that were very therapeutic, and I had discovered that *spirituality* was a huge, hidden world, which I had barely touched the surface of. This was exciting to me. It propelled me forward to new adventures instead of getting stuck and wallowing in my old pain.

During the beginning of spring in Aspen, the ice and snow are melting and the once beautiful little village turns into sludge, mud, and pools of water. Locals leave during this time of the year and take their vacations. They close their stores after the hectic winter months, take a break, and go away for a while. So it was a good and natural period in which to leave, together with everybody else during the lull. I said my silent good-byes and my eternal gratefulness for what it had given me. I wished it well as I drunk in my final mental pictures of the incredibly beautiful landscape as the three of us wound our way out of the valley along the narrow, twisting road toward California and a new beginning.

Discovering California

I loved California. The weather was wonderful and just what I was looking for. I found the people a bit disconnected compared to what I was used to, but in my case, this disconnection gave me space not be bothered while I progressed with my healing. One thing Californians don't do is interfere with your life. They leave you alone, which allowed me to feel that I could begin to spread my wings without causing some fuss for the first time in my life. I was able to enjoy the feeling of freedom, experimenting and learning without anybody being the least bit perturbed about it. It was a wonderful, liberating feeling! After a short time in California, I found employment and fell in love with someone from work. The girls left California to return to Colorado after three months. I moved in with a new boyfriend and lived with him for a year until I could tolerate him no more.

The very unfortunate thing about domestic abuse trauma survivors is that they tend to reenact their dysfunctional home lives. Where could we learn the healthy way? PTSD is a disorder that tends to repeat the traumas over and over again. So while my boyfriend was, on the surface, a magnificently handsome, talented, and successful person, at home he was an alcoholic and drug addict. We spent our time at home passionately. He took me out to wonderful places and beautiful dinners, but he could never stop the drinking or the uppers to get him through the day. I also quickly discovered that he could not keep his hands off other women either. What began as a relationship of such promise quickly turned into another nightmare, and I felt victimized again. I wanted to go back to South Africa and get away from the pain. This was my first relationship since my marriage, and I was devastated at the way it had turned out. I packed my things and returned to my home country. It was a trip that would change my life forever.

Enlightenment, Literally!

The moment I stepped off the plane in South Africa I knew I had made a mistake. The humid sea air struck me immediately, and with it, came an avalanche of associative, negative emotions. So the moment I could, I started to look for work so I could earn the airfare back to America. The coast notoriously does not pay very much money in the way of salaries, so I very quickly looked to move back to Johannesburg and back to my old job. Fortunately, they rehired me, and I moved once again. This time, I lived in a residential hotel not far from the central city hotel, so I could walk to work.

My very dear friend from college lived there with her husband. We had kept in touch over the years and were excited to see each other again. While I lived in Aspen, she had told me she'd gotten very involved with a spiritual group through her new husband. She offered to take me to one of their meetings if I ever came back to Johannesburg. At this point, I was very open to spiritual discovery, so once I got settled at work, we made arrangements to attend my first meeting with them to see what this spiritual path was all about. I was not prepared for the experience that awaited me at all!

I remember that they picked me up in this little sports car, which we all scrunched into as we drove to a commercial building somewhere in downtown Johannesburg. We went by elevator to a higher floor and then entered a room full of people. I can best describe it like this: it was the peaceful atmosphere in the room that struck me immediately in a very powerful way. Some people were seated on chairs, but some were comfortably seated on the floor, legs crossed and covered in eastern shawls. The feeling in the room was extraordinary! It was so incredibly serene yet amazingly powerful and spiritual. I had never felt anything like it. It felt immediately to me that this was the feeling and atmosphere I wanted to experience always in a spiritual sense.

Most in the room appeared to be meditating until the speaker of the meeting arrived and sat at a table to talk for an hour. I cannot remember a word that was said that day. I only know my body began to vibrate from head to toe. Outwardly, I could see no shaking, but every part of my body was vibrating furiously. It almost felt like an excitement, like my soul recognized something and was joyfully acknowledging it. This feeling did not end when the meeting ended but continued until it began to scare me a little. I had no frame of reference to inform me what this was, so while most went to lunch afterward, I had a great need to return home and try to assimilate all the sensations I was feeling.

I remember entering my little flat and feeling thirsty. I went to the bathroom faucet, turned it on, and cupped my hands to take a drink of cold water. As I bent over to take my first sip, it seemed like my entire forehead exploded open into pure white light. My natural eyes were blinded by the light, but an inner seeing took place. In the center of my forehead, there appeared an old Indian gentleman dressed in Persian clothing who just gazed at me intensely and then faded away. This experience was so profound and so extremely shocking to me that I immediately called my friends and frantically told them what I had just experienced. I begged them for an explanation. This light was so loving and bright. It was what I had read about in holy books and what people sometimes see in near death experiences. But I was not expecting to have such a personal and spontaneous experience after a spiritual meeting! My reaction to this event was even more interesting. My forehead seemed to stay open for another three days in which I continuously saw white light. I immediately wanted to meditate and lost all taste and desire for meat of any kind. I simply could not eat it anymore.

Of course, for this group, this was not so unusual an event. If it was a sign that this was my spiritual path to follow, I had received very powerful confirmation! I had never felt so spiritual and at peace. I borrowed all the books I could from my friends in order to educate myself on this new eastern philosophical path while I stayed in Johannesburg. I attended many more meetings and began to school myself on what this path was all about. In my healing from trauma process, this became my foundation. I learned about many new universal truths that I was previously unaware of. Discovering information about karma and the laws of karma became one of my greatest healing tools. To me, it is really the only thing that makes sense of the traumatic suffering some of us must endure especially at the hands of others. Those who feel that they did not deserve a traumatic event and are confused as to why they had to go through such an awful experience should read and educate themselves about the laws of karma. It was enormously helpful and healing for me! Finally, I understood.

Eventually, I returned to America. Again, I had learned so much in a short space of time. I felt more balanced and not so lost. The eastern philosophies are based on thousands of years of knowledge and firsthand writings of saints and spiritual masters who are all consistently saying the same thing. It gave me a wonderful, strong foundation—one that life had not given to me but rather taken away. My family background was shaky at best and not the least bit secure. My first venture out of my immediate family (my marriage) fared no better and left me in fear and confusion. Physically liberating myself from my past was very therapeutic. Spending time in Aspen was very healing and enlightening on more than one front. The experience in South Africa was beyond words and far more than I was expecting from life. All these accumulative healing experiences enabled me to begin to feel some empowerment again and gain more confidence within myself. So when I arrived back in America, I was ripe for my next growing experience. I fell in love and tried marriage again. It was 1982.

My Second Marriage

Marriage felt good for me, because it made me feel secure. He was a strong man, and I felt supported by his strength. I knew without a doubt that he would take care of me no matter what the circumstances. But again, coming from the awful relationship example of my childhood, I chose badly and erroneously. He was a Vietnam veteran, but coming from South Africa, which was not directly involved in any wars, I was ignorant of the impact this experience has on these individuals. I quickly learned firsthand what the negative fallout of PTSD from war trauma is to family members.

I very badly wanted more children and a cohesive family again. I was blessed with two sons in quick succession. I also wanted very badly to get some education, so when my second son was a few months old, I applied and gained entry into one of the top design schools. I began to study interior design, which had always been a passion of mine. I went on to finish design school with a degree, but unfortunately, the stresses of family life were taking a toll on my husband. His drinking was increasing, and by the time I had finished school, he was using drugs as well. This made him very belligerent at some point in the evening, and if I was available to fight with, he would take this opportunity to do so. While he never physically harmed me, he did verbally. Emotionally, this was taking a toll on me and the two boys. By 1989, I'd had enough of the constantly high tension levels and the fighting and gave him an ultimatum. He had to get some kind of psychological help and stop the drinking and drugs, or we would no longer be a family.

We sold our house, took some of the profit, and traveled the whole western United States over a six-month period. We were trying to regroup and take some of the stress out of the situation. When I did not see much improvement and he was refusing to get any assistance, I took off alone with the boys until one day a couple of months later I got a phone call from my husband saying he was no longer drinking and wanted all of us to get back together. He seemed truly sincere, and I believed him.

On the rare occasions when he wasn't drinking, he was a wonderful man. We eventually found a large, beautiful piece of land out of the city atmosphere and spent the next five and a half years there. In the beginning, it was amazingly good. We all thrived there, enjoying so many of the treasures that country living offers. We were also away from all the stresses of a high-population area, which is not very conducive to those suffering from the condition of PTSD due to war traumas. By this time, I realized what he was suffering from, but the more I asked and encouraged him to seek help from somebody, the more he resisted. He again insisted that there was nothing wrong with him. There was nothing I could do. I felt completely helpless, because this was something he alone had to face and sort out.

On my personal odyssey to healing during this period, I took up martial arts. It was something I had always wanted to do, especially after the terrible fear I had felt during the physical abuse of my first marriage. I never wanted to feel that fear again! This was a wonderful step forward in confidence-building. Of course, being a mom, it took me a little longer, but I eventually gained my black belt. With it, I also gained mental training over the years of quiet, steel confidence and learned how to conquer fear. I highly recommend this as a therapy for all women and children, as well as men, to say nothing of the incredible physical conditioning and strengthening you gain from such an activity. For me, this was also very stress relieving during a very shaky period of my life when I felt everything was ready to fall apart once again. Also, I believe strongly this training may have saved my life in the end.

My husband's drinking returned within a year of our move to the country. I believe he tried to appease the demons, but his job was very stressful and required him to spend long hours in a truck on busy highways. He was very tense when he finally arrived home late at night and took this stress out on me. Our sex life became nonexistent, and our fighting and arguing increased. Things were definitely escalating in the wrong direction.

During this period, he would tell me each day that he wanted to kill me. "I'll put you six feet under!" he would yell at me each day. I did not take this very seriously, to be honest, because he'd never hit me. I merely accepted that he was venting. When these ugly arguments would take place, almost immediately after he walked in the door, my youngest son would start to cry. I was becoming very unhappy in the situation. In my own unhappiness and sexual frustration, I started an affair with a doctor whom I met while working in town. This did not help things at home, of course, but I was desperate for some kind attention, and my husband had made it clear therapy was not an option for him. It became blatantly clear to me that I was repeating the old family cycle I had endured as a child. What I could not understand is why, if I hated alcohol and its awful effects on family members, I consistently picked partners who drank. With this question in mind, I went to see another psychotherapist.

I sat in front of a fairly young male therapist who politely asked why I was there. I told him of my serious concern for my marriage and my repetitive selection of clearly unsuitable alcoholic mates. I wanted to know why I did this if it made me so unhappy. He looked at me awhile and said, "Well, that is an easy question to answer." He went on to explain that children of alcoholic parents have some mixed wiring in their brains that associates love with alcoholism. We grow up with parents whom we automatically love. But because they are also alcoholics and we grow up with them from birth, we unconsciously begin to associate the two together. As a result, when we fall in love, we are also looking for and are comfortable with the connection of love and the smell of alcohol. He explained it well and recommended some books to read on children of alcoholic parents. But when I walked out of his office, I was already cured. The moment he highlighted the mixed connection in my head, I was able to disconnect from it. I have never again been attracted to men who drink. In fact, it is now a very quick turnoff. It was definitely the best-spent psychotherapy session I have ever had!

It was just a matter of time before the domestic situation between my husband and I reached the point of no return. We had been married twelve years, and I felt exhausted, unhappy, and hopeless. I found myself in a bad situation with two young children who relied on us, which was very concerning. One evening as we were arguing, he did a backhand punch toward my face. Because of my martial arts training, I very quickly dodged the punch, and he hit the wall behind. I was completely shocked, as this was a first! He looked at the hole he'd left in the wall, looked back at me, and said, "That should have been your face!"

This immediately put me on guard, and I knew I was also in a dangerous situation with him. It was clear, for the first time, that he could seriously hurt me. He was a large, tall man and as strong as an ox, so I would not have fared very well in a physical fight with him. Things became decidedly tenser between us from that moment on. It was two weeks later when we finally drew the straw that broke the camel's back.

It was during yet another daily barrage of spitefulness and insults we were hurling at one another when he pulled out the loaded shotgun we kept for protection. He cocked it, released the safety catch, and aimed it three inches from my face. I was literally staring down the barrel of a twelve-gauge shotgun! I was completely stunned. I immediately realized I was in an extremely dangerous, life-threatening situation. My two sons were in the living room next door watching TV, and all I could think about was that this could not happen to them. I would be dead, but they would have to see the carnage. I could not let that happen to them.

I looked at my husband's eyes, which were glazed and definitely not present. I knew he was not at all in control of this situation, so I had to be. My martial arts training came flooding into my awareness. Instead of panicking, which I am quite sure would have led me to scream and become hysterical and may have caused him to pull the trigger, I became very calm and fearless in those moments. I instinctively realized he had to become present. I had to make him aware of the situation we were in. I gently called his name—once and then again a little louder—but I did not move at all. I could see him struggling to focus, and then I could finally see his eyes start to really see me. Softly, I asked him to put down the gun. At the same time, I very slowly and gently put my right hand up towards the barrel of the gun pointed at my face and deflected it away from me. He put down the gun at last and seemed appalled at what had just taken place.

He said he was having a blackout, which is common for those who suffer from severe PTSD. During a blackout, the person has no idea or memory of what he is presently doing. My husband apologized profusely and told me he would never harm me. I suggested we go to sleep and discuss it in the morning, because he was still inebriated. I dared not risk another episode. I went to bed that night utterly in shock, but I also knew it was over between us. The marriage was necessarily over for all our sakes, and I did not ever want to have him back in our home again. When we woke the next morning, we discussed this. I remember him crying and saying he did not want to lose his sons. This was such a sad tragedy, but I was insistent for our safety. He did not return. Several months later, we were legally divorced, and I found myself a single parent. It was 1994.

My Third Marriage

My single status did not last long. The man I had been seeing was very much pressuring me to get married. I wasn't sure about this. I didn't feel totally in love with him, but there were several attributes he possessed that worked in his favor. He was a professional businessman and was able to provide a good, secure lifestyle for me and my children. He seemed happy to accept my sons into the marriage, and, most importantly, he didn't drink or take drugs of any kind. He seemed calm, passive, and kind, and I could not find any evidence that he would be violent or jeopardize our safety in any way. With two children, I had to be practical and realistic, so I agreed. We married in August 1994.

But this, unfortunately, was yet another learning curve for me. While I was now definitely not attracted to men who relied on alcohol and drugs to get themselves through the day, I was unprepared for one who liked to control me with finances. He became difficult to trust. I hadn't previously experienced this. I ignorantly trusted him, and while he taught me much in the way of business and encouraged me to develop my own, he had no plans to share with me any assets we built together in the marriage. For example, he never put me on the title to the house we bought together two years into the marriage but always assured me that this was not a problem. When our house was eventually sold, however, he walked out of the escrow office with the entire, substantial profit in hand, despite an account he set up with me to split the profits fifty-fifty. The money simply disappeared.

I found out what had happened when our real estate agent called and urged me to call an attorney. He explained that my husband had just changed the escrow instructions and walked out with the entire profit from the sale of the house. I called my husband and gave him an ultimatum to return the 50 percent within ten days, or I was filing for divorce. When he never returned my portion of the very hard-earned personal work on our property, I filed for divorce. I bought another home, and my sons and I moved to this property. I was a single parent again. It was the year 2000.

The divorce took a year of bickering and five attorneys to work out. I found out in the process of divorcing him that during our marriage he had all his retirement funds, bank accounts, and investment account information sent to his work address. As a result, I had no access to any true dollar amounts to present to the attorneys. He claimed the home was all his because the small initial down payment had come from funds he had earned before our marriage, even though we had already been married two years when we bought it and were making far more money than before he married me. He, on the other hand, knew exactly what my business had been earning and took his 50 percent in the negotiations. In the end, even with him withholding his true financial information and worth, he still owed me a substantial amount. He offered to give me less than half of that. If I had wanted more, I would have had to take him to civil court, prove my case of fraud, and invest another two years in the squabble, which would have cost me dearly in legal fees and untold emotional stress. I decided to just take what he offered and walk away from him. It was an ugly scenario and wasn't worth all the negative aggravation. I had lost all trust in him anyhow and just wanted to move on with my life.

I have to say this was definitely a huge, valuable lesson for me. It also became very clear that I couldn't make good, sound judgments when it came to selecting husbands! This really bothered me, and it seemed I needed another kind of healing or purging of my past in order to get the relationship part of my life right. These divorces were extremely difficult emotionally and were just adding to my piles of trauma. I felt emotionally heavy. I believed that I needed healing on a much deeper level but didn't know where to find this. This healing information finally came to me in the year 2006 on a trip to South Africa. I had an epiphany that would change the course of my life entirely. By this time both of my sons had left home and one was studying at university. For the first time in a very long time I was able to pursue my personal interests freely.

The Amazing Epiphany

I had been in South Africa for about three months, and it was time to return to the United States. It was the night before I was leaving, and I was checking that everything was taken care of in my little flat, because I would not be returning soon. I was about to close the door in the small second bedroom when I had a vision that appeared quite suddenly. I saw a massage table in the middle of the room, and there was a child lying on the table whom I was working on with my hands.

I had been to massage school many years ago. I'd earned most of the credits needed to become a massage therapist but had never finished the certification. I had worked for several years in massage as a massage technician, and knew enough about various massage techniques to acknowledge that the way I was touching the child was a technique I did not recognize at all. I watched fascinated and asked my inner self what technique or what modality this was that I saw myself practicing. I got a one-word answer: trauma. Still not understanding exactly what I had seen but clearly imprinted inside my memory, I returned to America.

On this particular trip, I had been very ill with stomach problems—not once but three occurrences, which had left me very drained of energy and concerned about my health. I returned to the United States in January 2007 and had no further occurrence until the following month. In February, however, I had another event, which was far more severe than the previous three. It put me in bed for two weeks to recuperate.

I was too weak to do much other than lie in bed and gather my strength during this time. My mind began to drift back to the vision I had received in South Africa. I asked my inner self again what I had seen in this vision. Again, I was told that it had to do with trauma and that I was to research the internet and discover what the technique was when I was a little better. I was now intrigued! As soon as I felt stronger, I did exactly that and found some interesting modalities that served as therapies for trauma survivors. It wasn't until I read about Trauma Touch Therapy and the description of the modality, however, that I thought I recognized what I had seen myself doing in the vision. I was so excited to discover this!

I immediately contacted the school in Colorado and found out that the course could only be taken after completing the credits necessary to become a massage therapist. I decided to go back to massage school and complete my certification. Then, I would go and learn this new technique. And that's what I did. I completed the unfinished credits of the two-year course by the end of 2007 and was enrolled to study Trauma Touch Therapy in the spring of 2008. I was very excited!

Training in Lakewood, Colorado

When the time came, I bought my air ticket to Colorado and booked a room at a nearby Holiday Inn for a week. I was headed to Lakewood, Colorado—specifically, the Colorado School of Healing Arts. The Trauma Touch Therapy program can be taken two ways—as a three-month course or, for those coming to study from out of state, as an intensive one-week course. The intensive is offered twice a year and is a blessing for those of us who are interested but cannot possibly spend three months in Colorado.

When they say intensive, they mean intensive! It's probably not the best way to take this particular course, as most in the room were also survivors of trauma. The technique releases old chronic trauma from all the cells and tissues of the body, so you can only imagine what was taking place in the training room! We started early in the morning and left late at night. We crammed three months of work into five days. We not only had the technique performed on us during this time but also learned how to treat others.

Trauma Touch Therapy is the brain child of a massage therapist and educator by the name of Chris Smith. Very wisely, she is the only one allowed to teach it. It is taught nowhere else in the world, and it is magnificent in construction. Chris Smith herself is a survivor of incest and a subsequent cancer survivor. In her own quest for healing and after studying other modalities dealing with trauma, she developed this very unique healing modality by integrating several techniques with very thoughtful construction, taking into consideration the very specific needs of those suffering from the aftereffects of trauma and chronic PTSD. Although the learning was rushed because I took it as an intensive course, I was grateful this made it possible to learn.

My trauma released very intensely one day in the middle of the training. We were enacting various psychotherapeutic terms, when during one these exercises, I felt an uncontrollable urge to flee out of the room. My fight-or-flight response had been triggered for a seemingly unknown reason, and all I could think of was running as fast as I could out of that training room. This seemed so illogical under the circumstances that I tried to stay put where I was as long as possible. Finally, I could control the feeling no longer and fled to the quiet of the closest bathroom. Once safely in one of the stalls with the door locked, I inexplicably broke down in tears. I sat crying and releasing for the next five minutes until I felt I had control of myself again, and then proceeded to wash my face of the tears and straighten up before returning to rejoin the class.

In the meantime, Chris Smith, who is ever vigilant while teaching, had sensed that something was not right with me. She sent one of her teaching assistants, a fully trained and certified Trauma Touch Therapist, to find me and check on me. It was a good thing she did! As I was rounding the corner from the bathroom to the classroom, the second wave of the release hit. Right at this moment, the TA met me in the hallway. It is difficult to describe what it felt like. I was crying again but harder, and it felt like a powerful freight train was about to explode out of my body, and then it did.

I felt nauseated and terrified. I wanted to throw up, my knees were beginning to buckle, and I began to dissociate and close my eyes. It felt so powerful and overwhelming that my need to escape was very intense. Simultaneously, I had a flashback to when I was an infant. I was lying on my back and became aware that I was too young to even turn myself in any way. I clearly saw a light on the ceiling in an old apartment we used to live in when I was a child. I was not seeing what was being done to me, but I felt terrified! I believe that this was the first time I had experienced trauma. Trauma Touch Therapy had brought me there to a place I could never previously remember in my conscious mind or ever talk to a therapist about, since this was a preverbal experience.

When you experience trauma during the preverbal years, how can you possibly resolve it when you don't have conscious memory of the event or how to describe it? So I felt this was a huge step forward in my healing. The TA instantly recognized my symptoms and applied what we call Emotional 911, bringing me *present* very quickly. After that, we did a special breathing technique to bring me into a parasympathetic state. The nausea subsided immediately, I calmed down again, and then she took me for a walk around the school until I felt more balanced and integrated. I was surprisingly calm after such a huge emotional release and attribute this to the quick application of Emotional 911, but I also felt quite exhausted. Chris allowed me to miss the afternoon session and sent me back to the hotel to sleep for a while. When I awoke, I had never felt better! It felt like a huge weight had been lifted off me. I felt light, happy, joyous, and ready to return to my studies early that evening, which I did.

I left Colorado a very different person from the one who had arrived five days earlier. I felt happy and content. I had learned a technique that I now knew from personal experience really worked for survivors still suffering the aftereffects of trauma. When your body is still full of negative emotions, you feel heavy and stuck. It is a hopeless feeling when, on a daily basis, you are overwhelmed by the normal stresses of life and are unable to control triggering, outbursts of anger, and subsequent dissociation.

Being controlled by negative emotions is exhausting and depressing. Personal relationships suffer enormously as a result. Drinking alcohol and taking drugs to numb the brain and the neurological system are often common to survivors as a desperate measure to control the beast that now rules their lives. Suicide is often seen as the only way out, further traumatizing the lives of loved ones. It is a vicious cycle. No matter how much you work on the mind in psychotherapy or how well your physical body heals, if the body cells and tissues are not also cleared of the negative emotions at the cellular level, the conditions and symptoms of PTSD only deepen and worsen and become more chronic.

PTSD is to be taken very seriously. It is a condition that gets worse with time if it remains untreated. The saying "time heals all wounds" does not apply to PTSD. This insidious condition definitely worsens with time and often symptomatically manifests physically as chronic illness or disease and sometimes ends in suicide. At the very least, it can so severely stunt the quality of life for a survivor that decades are lost in fear, poor decisions, a lack of healthy boundaries, lack of joy/thriving, loss of empowerment, and, sadly, lost opportunities to achieve personal hopes and dreams. Most trauma survivors that have not had sufficient healing also leave behind a trail of broken and disappointing personal relationships. This is not a way to live a life. This is hell. By sharing my own personal path to healing and my personal discoveries along the way, I hope that others will be encouraged to take assertive action, use some suggestions to gain back their lives, and take control again!

I continued studying with Chris Smith and completed the second half of the Trauma Touch Therapy training, which included the clinical section of the training, to become a Certified Trauma Touch Therapist. I started practicing in 2008. It is now my pleasure to be able to share all that I have learned on the subject over the years during my own healing process as a trauma survivor and now also as a therapist. I hope to perhaps educate, empower, and encourage you to do the same—to slowly but surely claim back your life from trauma, and thrive!

FOUR

What Is Trauma Touch Healing?
A Vital Missing Link Explained

Trauma Touch Healing is a very unique somatic touch therapy that specifically treats the deep, negative, emotional aspect of trauma. It assists a client in releasing these emotions from the cells and tissue of the body. This aspect has long been under appreciated and skipped over in treating those suffering from the aftereffects of trauma and PTSD. Physicians are trained to treat and assist survivors heal from any physical injury they may have incurred. Any subsequent treatment after the body has healed should involve the psychologist or psychiatrist to gain some intellectual understanding of what happened during the trauma experience and help balance the mind. This necessary mental balance calms some of the inevitable fears, guilt, depression, anxiety, anger, or rage a survivor may feel after the trauma. A psychologist may refer a patient to the psychiatrist for medications if they assess that it is necessary.

All of these initial therapeutic steps are usually necessary, initially, to bring health and mental stabilization to the survivor. It is after these two initial treatments that there has, for far too long, existed a gap in treatment. After these two treatments, when we feel we still need further help, who treats us next? Should we be satisfied to remain a survivor? Is it really possible to get back our former lives and thrive again? Go from survivor to thriver? Yes! It is possible. This is where Trauma Touch Healing comes into the picture.

In order for survivors to get from surviving to thriving, there must continue to be a forward movement in healing. Talk groups are very good therapy at this point, because a survivor usually has a strong need to discuss the trauma soon after the experience and a desire to connect with other similar trauma survivors. But this also has its limits, and sooner or later, a survivor will feel "talked out" and will start to look elsewhere for therapy. The natural, organic progression toward healing from trauma usually has survivors starting to crave touch at this point, with a strong growing feeling that the body also needs some kind of resolution. So survivors will attempt to seek out a body-worker therapist who can assist them unload the growing feelings of physical/emotional heaviness and uncomfortable feelings of being stuck and unable to move forward in life. This is a very frustrating state to stay in.

Survivors will now realize how much the trauma has negatively impacted their daily lives, will feel like they are now unable to live the kind of successful lives they know they potentially could be leading, and will fully realize that they are feeling disempowered to reach their personal goals. By the chronic stage, trauma has wound itself into the body tissue as well as the mind, and PTSD has settled in. While in its clutches, most energy each day is spent looping in between the trauma memory, triggering, dissociation and trying to get present again. Therefore with PTSD, there is often very little leftover time or energy for focusing on personal achievements and moving forward in life. Some trauma survivors emotionally give up at this point and are in very real danger of suicide because of the feelings of helplessness and hopelessness. Because of the poor emotional state of survivors at this juncture, chronic emotion-based physical problems are also surfacing.

And here lies the confusion. Who do you go to for treatment at this point? You quickly discover that treating the physical symptoms, whether by mainstream or alternative medicine, isn't doing much to permanently alleviate the somatic problems. Why? Because when a physical problem is a manifestation of deeply rooted negative emotions, it cannot heal from only treating the physical body. The root cause must obviously first be recognized, addressed, and healed before there can be a physical resolution. This is where Trauma Touch Healing is invaluable.

If any of the above is sounding familiar, this is an excellent time to go see a Trauma Touch Healer. This is the specialty of the modality—assisting the chronic PTSD client to unload the emotional, negative cellular memory from the physical body in a safe, slow, organic process. To heal completely from trauma, this process has to be done. As long as trauma memory remains held in the body tissue, a survivor develops more and more physical and emotional problems over time. It must be let go of!

PTSD has to earn our greatest respect, because it is one of those condi-

What Is Trauma Touch Healing? A Vital Missing Link Explained

tions that does not improve with time. It only gets worse and worse. The combination of daily surfacing trauma memory, subsequent triggering, and the resultant dissociation causes a re-victimization and re-traumatization cycle. Because the neurological system and the emotions are tied together, as trauma is repeatedly experienced, the chemicals and electrical charges are again and again shot into the body to prepare it for fight-or-flight, which is further recorded and stored in every cell in every part of the body. So if each day more and more negative emotional memory is being stored in the cells and if these charges are not being released out of the body, they will obviously compound inside. Over time, the trauma and negative emotions increase and gradually build up, becoming more deeply embedded and threatening to create imbalance and what we call dis-ease (or disease) within the body.

When homeostasis (the body's natural inclination to maintain balance) is compromised as the body becomes overwhelmed and threatened, it also weakens the immune system and can cause chronic physical conditions, illnesses, and diseases. These are sometimes life-threatening conditions that take hold in a weakened body. It is essential that these negative emotions do not continue to increase and be held repressed in our bodies but rather released out for personal health reasons, as well as overall emotional and psychological well-being.

Trauma is not a purely physical event. It is not a purely mental event. It is a deeply emotional body/mind/spirit event. It is a severe and overwhelming experience. In order to successfully treat trauma, all aspects of it must be clearly understood. To understand what happens to us during trauma, we must first explain the neurological system and what changes are made in the body when it's suddenly subjected to a traumatic event. To get a clear picture, the limbic system of the brain must be understood. The limbic system is that part of the brain that is impacted and reacts to traumatic events. In simple terms, the limbic system controls our primitive/emotional center. If we take a closer look into this system, including its various parts and their functions in the brain, we begin to understand how trauma, and especially repeated traumas, negatively impacts us. We will also better understand the condition called PTSD.

When confronted by excessive stress internally or externally, our immediate physiologic response is the fight-or-flight response. What is the fight-or-flight response? It is a body's automatic, primitive, hard-wired brain response that prepares the body to fight or flee from a perceived threat or attack for our survival. When the fight-or-flight response is triggered, a sequence of nerve cell firings occurs, and chemicals like adrenaline, noradrenaline, and cortisol are released into the bloodstream. This causes the body to go through a series of dramatic changes. Some of these changes include muscular changes preparing the body to fight or flee, which is a direct result of blood being diverted away from the digestive system and sent to the muscles and limbs, which will require extra energy/fuel for fighting or running. Also, awareness intensifies, pupils dilate, sight sharpens, impulses quicken, and the perception of pain diminishes. All of this prepares the body physically and psychologically for fight-or-flight and moves us into an attack mode.

When our fight-or-flight response is activated, our perception is that everything in our environment is a threat to our survival. It bypasses the rational and logical mind and moves us into a primitive attack mode for our survival. In this mode, we may overreact to the slightest sound, fear is exaggerated, thinking is distorted, and we are alert to any possible danger. Our focus narrows to concentrate on things that can harm us. Therefore, fear becomes the way we perceive the world.

If a trauma is severe enough or somebody experiences multiple traumas (war veterans, victims of long-term childhood abuse, domestic abuse victims, or victims of torture, etc.), the fight-or-flight response can become stuck or frozen. If somebody perceives an overwhelming threat is so great, the physiology shuts down the system and can stimulate a permanent state of hyper-arousal, staying frozen in the fight-or-flight response. These responses occur when survival mechanisms are activated to keep the physiology on constant special alert.

Dr. Bessel van der Kolk, who has written many articles on trauma and authored *Psychological Trauma,* a book frequently used by therapists who work with trauma survivors, describes manifestations of traumatic psychobiology as the following: "In an apparent attempt to compensate for chronic hyper-arousal, traumatized people seem to shut down.... Thus, people with chronic PTSD tend to suffer from numbing of responsiveness to the environment, punctuated by intermittent hyper-arousal in response to conditional traumatic stimuli." He further notes, "What distinguishes people who develop post traumatic stress disorder from people who are merely temporarily overwhelmed, is that people who develop PTSD become 'stuck' on the trauma, keep re-living it in thoughts, feelings or images. It is this constant, intrusive "reliving"—not the actual trauma—that causes PTSD."

What Is Trauma Touch Healing? A Vital Missing Link Explained

At this point, we will further discuss what changes occur in the brain of a survivor with post traumatic stress disorder. During the experience of trauma, incoming sensory information is first sent to the thalamus, which is involved in sensory perception and regulation of motor functions and plays an important role in the relay and integration of information and chemical releases. The fight-or-flight response is processed in an area called the hypothalamus, which, when stimulated, initiates a sequence of nerve cell firings and chemical releases into the body preparing it for fight-or-flight.

Information and chemicals are then relayed to the amygdala, a tiny, nut-sized part of the brain that exists in both hemispheres. The amygdala is directly responsible for emotional processing within the nervous system. It interprets sensory information as potentially threatening, unusual, or otherwise significant and then initiates behavioral and psychological responses (fight-or-flight). A very important role of the amygdala is that it creates emotional memories. However, this center is very sensitive, is prone to irritability, and is easily agitated. During repeated trauma (or triggering), this center becomes suspect to regular chemical flooding, which becomes corrosive to the amygdala over time. It then remains in a state of chronic irritation and overreaction.

From the amygdala, information is forwarded to the hippocampus, a very big player of neurological emotions. The hippocampus neurologically associates and consolidates incoming sensory information and disseminates it to different areas of the brain to be stored as memory. (It sorts experiences out.) It also creates associations between past and present experiences to create appropriate responses. The hippocampus is also very vulnerable to disruption and stress, which cause it to shrink in size and diminish in function. This diminished function subsequently prevents the hippocampus from sending the proper responses to the frontal cortex (that part of the brain behind our foreheads) where memory is normally stored and organized for clear reasoning.

As a result, a person with PTSD sometimes cannot see the difference between past and present experiences. Therefore, logical thinking can no longer take place. A perfect example of this is a military person returned to a non-war situation (home) who is walking in a supermarket when somebody there drops something heavy, creating a large bang. The military person could immediately trigger from the loud, sharp sound and flash back to a similar-sounding, traumatic wartime experience. In an instant, the sound in the present is associated with the sound in the past. As a result, the person reacts as if he were presently there. To a nonmilitary person just shopping, this appears illogical and crazy, because they are aware that the soldier is no longer in a war situation. Therefore, the spectator may find it very difficult to understand why the soldier would react in such a manner.

Well, hopefully, we can now better understand these spontaneous, uncontrollable responses that survivors struggle with each day. Surprisingly, I have also treated clients who did not understand their own reaction and lack of clear reasoning when triggering and under duress, despite having undergone extensive psychotherapy. They too thought they were crazy and felt highly embarrassed by these responses. Yet, they had never been given any tools or techniques to gain control of the triggering or dissociation. I am really not sure how a client can spend years in psychotherapy receiving treatment for trauma and yet emerge from treatment still so ignorant of his own condition. Most of my clients, well familiar with experiencing triggering and dissociation, have never heard the word dissociation, know what it means, or realize that they even do it after years of psychotherapy. I know, because I ask them this question in my intake. From what they tell me, it was simply never explained. (Dissociation, a response that causes one to space out or go mentally to another place more pleasant than the trauma, is explained in more detail in the next chapter.)

Continuing, from the hippocampus information is then sent to the frontal cortex. Within the frontal cortex, the neocortex is the frontal lobe associated with planning, reasoning, and the ability to initiate voluntary action and responses. The prefrontal cortex associates past with present experiences relevant to the current situation. This is known as *working memory*. Trauma Touch Healing, through a unique method of reversing the trauma spiral back out of the body while assisting and teaching a client how to release the stored traumatic negative emotional charges and memories from cells and body tissue, subsequently restores working memory (for clear logical reasoning). This happens as the neurological system begins to repair itself.

This process happens very quickly with Trauma Touch Healing. I have treated clients who start treatment feeling mentally cloudy or muddled in the forehead area and who complain they really struggle to think in a clear, focused way when they need to. After about four to five weeks of treatments, these same patients tell me their frontal lobes are already beginning to have clarity, a sense of clearness, and mental organization, and they begin to excitedly feel in control of themselves again. For the therapist, this is a wonderful

What Is Trauma Touch Healing? A Vital Missing Link Explained

process to watch unfold—watching actual, real, practical progressive healing taking place. Real results! It's very similar to watching a birth.

So we can see that it's almost impossible to cultivate positive attitudes and beliefs when stuck in survival mode and caught in the cycle of post traumatic stress disorder. To protect ourselves, we close off our emotions. Our clear reasoning is disconnected to the point that it becomes impossible to make clear choices or recognize the consequences of those choices. It is never good when our consciousness is focused on fear. When we are focused on short-term survival and then overwhelmed with daily stressors, a survivor's life just becomes a miserable series of short-term emergencies. (You will notice there is always lots of drama surrounding trauma survivors, especially in their personal relationships.) Since closing off feelings in an attempt to numb negative emotions is not selective, all emotions are closed off, even positive ones such as happiness and joy. Living from one crisis to another as a way of life, with an absence of joy as a counterbalance, quite soon results in burnout and depression. It is usually at this point that a survivor begins to look for some real solutions. When the desire to change your life for the better supersedes any fear you may have to step out of the safety zone of staying comfortable (also called being emotionally stuck), this is the right moment to seek Trauma Touch Healing.

The way PTSD symptoms form as they energetically wind their way in a clockwise direction deeper into the body after a trauma is an interesting process. Trauma Touch Healing calls it the Trauma Vortex. Over time, survivors get more and more deeply entrenched into this cyclic vortex where life choices become very limited. The losses we experience after trauma are extensive. The initial symptoms are disempowerment, a loss of speaking out (confidence is too shaken), loss of boundaries (loss of sense of self), loss of the wild instinctual nature you possessed beforehand, loss of choices, and then, of course, an inevitable sense of hopelessness. Mentally, we now feel like victims and have developed strong feelings about this negative change when the realization sets in that the trauma was unavoidable and completely out of our control. With this realization, victims begin to feel a great deal of rage.

The second phase is the mental embodiment of the victimization belief system. The survivor begins to assume the status of a victim. With this strong change in mental beliefs, there is also a strong shifting of perception of the self in relationship to the world. We now view ourselves very differently. We see ourselves as victims instead of as confident, thriving individuals.

Following this important change in mental perspective is the somatic (physical) embodiment of the feelings of victimization. The mind-over-body concept is now seen at work. In this phase of the cyclic vortex, the body tissue begins to adapt to the belief system/perceptions being experienced mentally, and the experiences/history is now being steadily embodied. As a result, the soma becomes armored, dense, collapsed, etc. During this phase, many physical symptoms and illnesses develop, including diseases. This is a phase where treatment of physical ailments and symptoms has little effect, because the *root cause* is not physical but emotional.

Once the trauma experience is embodied mentally, physically, and emotionally, we begin the phase of being stuck in the trauma mode. We begin to loop over and over, repeating the trauma cycle. Here begins the unhealthy reengagement in dysfunctional relationships/lifestyles—a repeating of similar situations that reflect the primary trauma scenario. This, unfortunately, feels comfortable because it is what is known and what has now become familiar. At this point, many survivors find it too scary to make the changes back to what was and often stay stuck in the victimization mode by choice.

If a survivor keeps reengaging in the primary trauma scenario as we discussed above, this causes re-traumatization and re-victimization. The cycle is repeated all over again, reinforcing the dysfunctional belief system that now amplifies the somatic fixation. With this cyclic repetition of the original trauma over and over, a survivor's condition becomes worse and worse over time.

The cyclic vortex described above is a natural progression for survivors of trauma. We are neurologically hardwired to respond this way to trauma. How we react to a trauma may be different from person to person, but the basic pathway to developing PTSD is a predictable one and does not vary depending on the type of trauma. In other words, this same cycle will develop whether the person is a victim of a car accident, an injury, war trauma, or childhood abuse. The really crucial question is this: once you have developed the chronic condition of PTSD and are now caught in this depressing and frustrating cyclic vortex, how can it be reversed out of the body successfully? What is a solution?

Trauma Touch Healing utilizes a unique process whereby the therapist uses his skills while shifting the patient's focus to recognize the varied body/mind responses that can occur with trauma. The intent of Trauma Touch Healing is to create a safe and nurturing environment to slowly explore healthy touch with lots of emotional space and investigating sensation and feeling in the body while releasing negative emotions from the body tissue. Arriving at the place where this is possible takes time and patience. It also requires trust on the part of the client. Knowing our boundaries is crucial if we are to be working with trauma. To maintain integrity, clients are requested to be or have been involved in some kind of therapeutic process. A holistic attitude toward healing is also encouraged, integrating the physical self with therapeutic touch, psychoanalysis, and spirituality.

When touch releases old issues, there is a great potential in the moment to break through and transform somatic patterns around the trauma. Then the body/mind is reeducated and integrated to learn new ways of being and reacting, taking the negatives experienced in trauma and turning them into something of value. Empowering a victim of trauma to thrive again, rather than just survive, is the goal of Trauma Touch Healing. It also assists clients in redirecting the energy they are normally forced to use as they struggle to cope with negative emotions. This redirection transmutes the common feelings among survivors of helplessness and powerlessness to positive action. When the body/mind/spirit has been reconnected and integrated, this new balanced energy can now be preferably used to move forward in life to achieve personal hopes and dreams that had previously been put on hold by being stuck in the trauma cyclic vortex.

Trauma Touch Healing is the only body/mind/spirit therapy I know that deals with trauma healing in a truly comprehensive way. PTSD is a complicated and often dangerously fragile, unstable condition that should never be handled by people who have had neither the training nor education to cope with it—period.

The Trauma Touch Healing modality is narrowly focused toward a reversal of the trauma cyclic vortex, which spirals in a counterclockwise direction out of the body. Through its unique, innovative, somatic, and highly effective techniques, this therapy achieves the following:

A client discovers that the first step is waking up from the trance. Here the survivor begins to consciously recognize the negative patterns they adopted and now becomes uncomfortable with them. As the ten-week course of therapy progresses further, the client begins to express a healthier self-image. At this point, the client regains their voice and begins to name and shift relationships, establishing safety and developing a healthy sense of boundaries. The third step involves unraveling the psychosomatic armoring. The unwinding of trauma occurs here with the actual hands-on manipulation of body tissue. As somatic memories and holding patterns begin to unravel, the trauma is finally uncoupled or disconnected with the therapeutic use of natural sensations in the body.

After this occurs, there is also an intellectual transformation. Old beliefs fall away, and the mind cannot hold onto the old tapes as easily. Definite shifts in perception occur, and the survivor exits this cycle with empowerment and a sense of unlimited potential. Trauma Touch Healing calls this healing vortex *Soul Infusion*. This is an unwinding healing spiral where one is able to organically surrender old beliefs, attitudes, and relationships that are no longer vital in order to embody the soul's birthright. It's important to always remember that despite overwhelmingly negative experiences we are sometimes forced to endure in life, wholeness is still our birthright!

I quote from a professional development article called "Trauma Touch Therapy" written by Chris Smith, a CMT from Colorado and developer of this therapy for *Touchstone Journal*:

> *I have often said that it takes the courage of a warrior to embark on the long and difficult journey of healing our trauma. For those of us who have survived trauma and abuse, the idea of living in a body full of feelings, full of sensations, memories, thoughts and pictures, can be terrifying. Simple acts of touch, movement and breath can produce a heightened level of activity in the body's nervous system, this activity is coupled with feelings of terror; these feelings are in turn, a reminder of the trauma. And so we numb ourselves, sometimes for years and years, until we resemble empty shells. No feelings, no aliveness, no ability to find joy in watching a beautiful sunset or respond to the touch of a loved one."* She further says, *"Psychotherapy provides one important avenue of self discovery and understanding; however there seems to be limitations as to the distance one singular approach can take someone on their journey towards healing. It can be frustrating to discover just how many layers there are to our wounds. Many of my clients report that after all the years of working with their trauma on a cognitive level, their minds feel more at peace but their bodies now want some resolution as well.*

What I personally love about Trauma Touch Healing is that it provides real, practical help, not only with releasing trauma from the body but also through a special breathing technique to stop and prevent triggering and get one *present*. An entire healing session is also dedicated to reestablishing boundaries in an energetic way (not by merely talking about it), and another session covers finding our joy center in the body, which helps enormously with those suffering depression from trauma and how to spiral out of it very quickly. This is why I have said it is a most comprehensive healing technique in the treatment of trauma. It is very highly and specifically focused to assist survivors cope with the negative symptoms they suffer from in PTSD.

If you have reached the point of seeking bodywork in the next step of your healing process and are considering a modality, I highly recommend asking your prospective therapist some important questions. This is especially important if you have a strong trauma history. The following can help protect against re-traumatization.

1. What is the therapist's education, especially regarding trauma?
2. How long is the intake? (It should be at least one hour.)
3. What techniques are offered to assist with triggering?
4. Can the therapist explain what dissociation is and how to control it?
5. What technique is given to reestablish boundaries?
6. What technique is offered to assist with depression?
7. Do they have a technique to control rage?
8. How does the therapist release the trauma from the body tissue (method)?
9. Is this technique also taught to the client?
10. Can the therapist explain how trauma affects the limbic system?
11. How is the therapy work integrated into the body?

If a bodyworker cannot answer all of these questions proficiently and satisfactorily, you are probably in the hands of a therapist with insufficient education/training to be even contemplating working on a client with emotional trauma-related issues. It is not advised to have an uneducated bodyworker perform treatment on you for trauma. You will only harm yourself more than you will help yourself, sometimes with serious consequences. If a therapist is unaware of re-traumatization caused by an emotional release combined with dissociation, they will hurt you instead of heal you. You will have also squandered your hard-earned resources unnecessarily! One of the great frustrations presently for everybody is that alternative medicine costs are rarely covered by insurance companies. If they are covered, it is usually for therapies that are not going to help you get proper, safe methods of emotional release. So what happens when you are now feeling so strongly that your body also needs resolution? Who do you go to? To ensure you get yourself to the correct therapist, personal education of the different modalities, their scopes and limits, and how they may contribute positively to your healing is your best defense. (See Chapter Ten.)

In my own experience, the most streamlined way to become healed from trauma is first the physician (which includes treatment and referrals to physical therapists, occupational therapists, specialists, surgery, etc.) and then the chiropractor for any neck/spine damage assessment and soft tissue treatments (may also include massage therapy) if necessary. When the body is healing sufficiently and when you feel the need, the psychotherapist is usually the next step to gain emotional balance and mental understanding of what happened to you. Everybody is different here, but when you feel that the therapist is no longer helping (as each modality has its limitations), have the courage to tell the psychotherapist that you are ending the therapy to move on.

Too many clients I have treated have been in psychotherapy for years and years, making very little progress. As they are voicing their frustrations to me during the intake, I always ask why they kept going so long if it was no longer helping. The answer is always that the psychotherapist just kept making the appointments week after week, month after month, year after year, often despite the client's feelings that they no longer felt served by the therapy. They, unfortunately, trusted the therapist's advisement rather than their own intuition. This is an easy mistake for a trauma survivor who feels so helpless. Being in psychotherapy for years with no referrals for proper somatic emotional release work has a very negative, long-lasting effect on a survivor of trauma.

The long period of time held in talk therapy allows the trauma to solidly wind into the body, creating all kinds of physical havoc (discussed above). The client has now also developed symptoms of PTSD with all its devastating effects. Without the correct body/mind/spirit resolution, a survivor begins to feel there is something wrong with them, because everybody has told them, untruthfully or ignorantly, that psychotherapy is the treatment that should eventually heal them from trauma. When it's obviously not completely healing the trauma and physical symptoms are only getting worse and worse, heavy depression often sets in with a good dose of feeling like a failure. I have had clients who told me they had begun to entertain serious thoughts of suicide when utter hopelessness at their situation was setting in and they could see no way out or anybody else to really help them. Often at this point, drugs from the psychiatrist are suggested as a solution! How can we continue to still be this ignorant?

Now we know that it takes many therapists to gain resolution for trauma, and when a survivor feels no longer served by a therapist, a client should move onto the next therapy. I often wonder at what point a psychotherapist finally refers a client to somebody else, other than a prescription writer, who can really be of help. Are they ignorant of other therapies out there? Not willing to refer for financial reasons? It is perplexing. I will say this: trust your own intuition on what you need and don't need! When you no longer feel served by a therapy, end it and move on. An unethical or ignorant therapist serving his own needs is only going to impede your healing progress with terrible consequences. Be the warrior and don't allow that to happen.

A natural next step to follow psychotherapy, or in conjunction with psychotherapy, is a body therapy that will somatically allow body tissue to release the heavy, negative emotions. It is useless and a waste of time and money going to any other bodyworker until the body tissue is cleared of the trauma at its deepest level within the body. In fact, not even a massage has a long affect on the body while it remains hostage to trauma memory trapped in the cells. First, clear the body of trauma, get all the techniques to control PTSD symptoms at your fingertips (which will allow the neurological system to heal), and learn how to release emotions immediately. My recommendation is Trauma Touch Healing, as it is the most comprehensive therapy I presently know that can safely provide victims and survivors with all the above and more.

A big problem you should be aware of when receiving trauma therapy from any bodyworker is the following: because of a lack of appropriate training, most bodyworkers are sadly unaware that an emotional release combined with dissociation leads to a re-traumatization of the client. When this occurs, as it often does with uneducated therapists, the client is badly emotionally hurt instead of helped.

A benefit of Trauma Touch Healing is that it reconnects and integrates you to your body. After this takes place, finding the next therapist to fulfill your healing needs will come much more easily than when your body was numbed out and you were disconnected from it. When a survivor is numbed out and has limited dialogue with their body, it becomes very confusing to navigate around the myriad of bodyworkers claiming to help one heal from trauma. Which really do and which don't? Because we are not getting clear guidance from mainstream medicine (physicians and psychotherapists), it is then particularly beneficial being reconnected and in touch with your own intuition and body again when selecting the next therapist. So logically, it makes more sense to first gain back your power with a cleared body together with empowering techniques to control PTSD symptoms. Then you can move on, feeling newly grounded and balanced with mental clarity, which all assist in decision-making.

According to Trauma Touch Therapy creator Chris Smith, quoted in an article written by Karrie Mowen for *Massage & Bodywork* magazine, "What started as an uncomplicated means to address trauma is now finding its place in the world of massage and bodywork. And it's working for clients." Smith describes the work as "extremely successful."

> *"I would really say it's 100% successful, because clients get to do the work they think they need to do," she said. "It's based on what goals the client comes in with. Do clients leave feeling more empowered? Yes. Do they have more autonomy and a sense of self-sufficiency? Absolutely. Can they experience their body more fully without dissociating? Yes." Smith said many of the clients she sees will report to her their twenty years of psychotherapy. "They'll say, 'I get it in my brain, but ...' That's where Trauma Touch Therapy comes in. By working with their traumas and by having the client identify how they've shut down and become numb, an 'aliveness' begins to seep through all the armoring that's taken place. That 'aliveness' is a magic pill of sorts, which begins waking the client into a new paradigm where they can begin living life again. It may sound simple, but that's what Trauma Touch Therapy is all about."*

Through experiencing my own healing process and being a therapist for others, I have discovered, and am convinced, that when it comes to the complicated conditions and symptoms of trauma, one cannot blindly leap from physicians and psychotherapists to alternative medicine healers without knowing exactly what you are doing and whom you are entrusting yourself to. Up till now, with regards to trauma healing, there has been a huge glaring void after mainstream medicine. The missing link, I have found, is that once the physical body is healed and the mind is balanced, there essentially must be a clearing out and letting go of the negative emotions from the tissues of the body first before any other bodywork can be beneficial. This is vital to understand. Having done a great deal of research and, again, from personal experiences, I can say with absolute confidence that Trauma Touch Healing is the best therapy for this particular purpose. Comparatively, it is the only bodywork therapy I presently know that is as focused and comprehensive and truly addresses all the urgent issues trauma survivors and those suffering from PTSD face on a daily basis.

It is true that up till now it has not been widely known. But now it is the year 2017, the year of changing paradigms, especially in the world of healing. The emergence of knowledge and secrets previously hidden or lying dormant are waiting to be discovered. I believe the missing link to successful trauma healing has been found!

FIVE

Cracking the PTSD Code!
The Positive Effects of Trauma Touch Healing

This chapter is an addition to my original book, *Secrets to Tame a Mystical Dragon*, which I published in 2012. It took years of practice before I received an extraordinary epiphany of exactly how the method I had learned to treat PTSD was positively affecting my clients and their brains, how it was reversing the condition, and why this method was having such a powerful healing effect on PTSD. In November 2016 I received a stunning moment of clarity. Suddenly my mind was opened to vital missing pieces of knowledge and understanding that I had been seeking for quite some time, and all the dots finally connected. In that moment of enlightenment I understood completely and can now clearly explain, not only in metaphysical terms (which was my initial approach), but more importantly also explain the therapy in physiological and scientific terms. This knowledge will reveal what the powerfully positive *effects* are of applying the unique Trauma Touch Healing method, and how it is achieved. It is, therefore, a great pleasure to share and release to the world for the very first time the following new and invaluable information.

PTSD is an incredibly complex condition. It brings with it such a dysfunction in body, mind and spirit that it often becomes the ruination of an entire life if left untreated. The value to any healer who really understands the benefits of knowing how to break the syndrome of PTSD, is taking a huge step forward and upwards to successfully treating their clients suffering from this insidious condition and being unable to disconnect from it. Once corrected, billions of individual lives could be brought back to normalcy and thriving, instead of struggling to barely survive. With this knowledge I imagine entire countries/societies, especially those who have endured prolonged negative conditions such as war or oppression, coming back to healthy life again. Once healthy, there is no limit to what these individuals can positively achieve. I have joyfully witnessed this in my own practice over the years with those I have treated. It has been a great privilege.

When the human body is emotionally overwhelmed by a traumatic event, it often requires assistance or an intervention to help correct the situation in order to heal and re-balance. Our bodies are constantly working to achieve a healthy state of balance, called *homeostasis*, whether we are aware of it or not. With PTSD the body is overwhelmed from unreleased trauma, and this creates a great pressure build up in the body, which then develops into an emotionally negative cycle in the brain. This causes the Emotional Brain (Limbic System) to become too dominant, presenting itself as an uncontrollable emotional imbalance. The problem in correcting or reversing this condition, and assisting the body to achieve an essentially healthy balance, is that almost nobody I have heard of, knows how to successfully treat it in totality. There are bits and pieces of treatments going on (symptomatic treating), but this does very little to fully reverse trauma, or release it completely from the body. I will explain why this is so as we go along.

Understanding the Basics of the Limbic System of the Brain: Mind

There are two main sections of the brain: 1) the NeoCortex which is the larger section, known as the Intelligent Brain, and 2) the Limbic System, the smaller of the two, known as the Emotional Brain. When dealing with PTSD, there is much talk about the Limbic System. This is a small, highly complex and important center in the middle of the brain just above the brain. Its job is to receive and respond to incoming data and information carried to the brain through the sensory neurons of the Peripheral Nervous System (PNS), which then sends it onto the Central Nervous System (CNS).

**Easy to remember: CNS = Spine and Brain,
and the PNS = everywhere else.**

The Limbic System processes the incoming information through its various parts, and after organizing it, sends the processed information to the Frontal Lobes (behind the forehead) to be stored for logical, clear, balanced reasoning when we need to think, and come to solutions in our daily lives

(Working Memory). The Limbic System is the part of the brain most affected by emotional, traumatic events. When the Limbic System receives information alerting it to danger, it immediately springs into action and floods the body with adrenalin. This powerful, potent chemical quickly changes the dynamics of the body to prepare it for "fight or flight": It diverts blood away from the stomach and increases blood flow to muscles and lungs, the muscles of the body tense to fight or flee, the heart rate increases, and the pupils dilate for better vision. It also provides vasodilation to the heart's coronary vessels, constricts the intestinal sphincters and urinary sphincter, and inhibits peristalsis. The body can achieve all of this in seconds.

When we are at such a high level of hyper-arousal, any readers who have experienced "fight or flight" will often remember the traumatic event happening in slow motion. Obviously the event was happening in "real time" but our bodies were operating at such a heightened super-speed to protect us from death or danger, the event seems to slow way down. Therefore, the event is being experienced in an altered state, and merely perceived as slowed down. Under *normal* circumstances once danger has passed, the body slowly releases the "fight or flight" electrical charges, and comes down from a "high" to a state of relaxation again (Sympathetic to Parasympathetic). This process to normalcy takes a few hours to achieve, usually four to five hours.

Here is an important key: There is *already* a natural system in place in the body that can gear up for trauma, but then release and relax when the imminent danger has passed. Under normal circumstances this process is achieved involuntarily, meaning that we don't have to force ourselves to do it, the body does it naturally for us. This wonderful gift is compliments of the Autonomic Nervous System (ANS). Hold that thought.

But what happens to this organic release process under abnormal circumstances such as chronic child abuse, domestic abuse, wars, torture, rape, and so on, where a single event is overwhelming, or there are repeated traumas often on a daily basis? When a human is subjected to multiple traumatic events (although a dramatic single event can definitely achieve the same result), the neurological system attempts to compensate. During extended periods of trauma, memory provides the information that sometime soon another trauma will follow, so under these circumstances the body maintains a state of hyper-arousal so it can more quickly to achieve "fight or flight." In these cases, it is not helpful to fully relax because of the vast amount of energy it takes for the body to get back into the state of hyper-arousal. In these kinds of scenarios the body stays in a semi-perpetual state of alertness, unable to fully relax, and always waiting for the next event. If this scenario continues, especially over extended periods of time, the Limbic System starts to dysfunction due to electrical charge overload, building pressure, and corrosive "fight or flight" chemicals, often becoming frozen in a "hyper" mode, and therefore stuck in a state of high alertness. Obviously this has negative repercussions over time, especially to the Limbic System. Why? Because it is here in the brain that the information is sent to counteract danger, and the response is to send adrenalin throughout the body to prepare it for "fight or flight." Adrenalin is an extremely powerful chemical that chronically, over time, does actual physical damage to parts of the Limbic System. Thus, when having to endure repeated traumas and triggering, not only does it cause this system to be unnaturally suspended in a state of "fight or flight," but it's also breaking down the Limbic System due to the chronic, caustic effects of this potent chemical which causes irritation and inflammation.

We were not designed to continually experience traumatic events such as abuse or war on a daily basis. We were beautifully designed and electrically (neurologically and energetically) pre-wired to receive, react, and then release trauma. One-time events. But when a human being remains continually held in a state of hyper-arousal, adrenalin is also constantly being sent into the body, keeping it tense, hypersensitive, and overreactive, especially when triggered. And since the Limbic System controls the Emotional Brain, emotions also become hypersensitive and overreactive. Importantly, there are serious negative repercussions to the Limbic System being habitually forced to release adrenalin. Let me explain why.

The complex Limbic System is made up of several parts. The major components are: the Thalamus, the Hypothalamus, the Amygdala, and the Hippocampus. Each of these parts has a different important function in the brain:

The Thalamus plays an important role in the relay and integration of incoming information and chemical releases (adrenalin).

The Hypothalamus, located just above the brain stem, acts as an integrator for autonomic functions, receiving ANS (Autonomic Nervous System) regulatory input from the Limbic System to achieve this.

The Amygdala is directly responsible for emotional processing within the nervous system. It interprets sensory information that is potentially threatening, unusual or otherwise significant, and initiates behavioral and psychological responses. One of its most important roles is creating emotional memories. However, it is prone to irritability, can get easily agitated, and is affected by chronic, corrosive chemical flooding. An inflamed, irritated Amygdala (causing dysfunction as a result), is not helpful, especially when we become aware of the importance of its role. This is not the only part of the Limbic System to be affected.

The Hippocampus is a very large participant of neurological emotions. It neurologically associates and consolidates incoming sensory information, disseminating it to different areas of the brain to be stored as memory. (In other words, it organizes our experiences). It also helps create associations between past and present experience to create appropriate responses. However, the Hippocampus is very vulnerable to disruption and stress, which causes it to shrink in size and diminish in function. This diminished function causes a failure in sending correct responses to the Frontal Cortex (behind the forehead), where memory is normally stored and organized for clear, logical reasoning, when required. The result of this for those suffering from PTSD, is that often a person appears confused and unfocused, unable to properly differentiate between past and present experiences (triggering), and therefore not much logical, clear thought can take place.

I cannot tell you how many clients I have treated who have expressed, at the beginning of therapy, that they feel "crazy" and "out of control." When trauma survivors tell you this, believe them—it is indeed true, as we can see from the above information. The good news is that the brain has great plasticity, and once the "stuck" traumas are naturally released from the body, the brain quickly re-wires and re-sets itself and begins its journey back to balance, health, and correct functioning. No more crazy! PTSD is not a permanent condition unless one fails to release the electrical charges and negative emotions created from trauma that over time leads to a high pressure build-up in the ANS, brain dysfunctions, and other trauma-related disorders and illnesses (*dis*-ease).

Remember this key: Under normal, healthy circumstances the Intelligent Brain and the Emotional Brain are in balance. However, due to the syndrome/cycle of PTSD, the Emotional Brain takes over and dominates the Intelligent Brain so intensely that focus, and good, clear, logical, rational thought are often very challenging for a trauma survivor to achieve.

Symptoms commonly experienced from PTSD include the following:

- Fear
- Anger
- Rage
- Depression
- Paranoia
- Anxiety
- Recurrent nightmares
- Terrorizing flashbacks
- Insomnia
- Panic attacks
- Cloudy thinking
- Shame
- Guilt
- Dread
- Despair
- Helplessness
- Lack of empowerment
- Unhappiness
- Substance abuse/addictions
- Moodiness
- Isolationism
- Uncontrollable weeping and grief
- Sweating
- Shaking and trembling
- Constant fidgeting and nervousness
- Physical weakness
- Chronic pain
- Dissociation
- Total physical and emotional collapse

All of the above are emotional and conditional symptoms which I am sure the reader agrees are very good to disconnect from!

Cracking the PTSD Code! The Positive Effects of Trauma Touch Healing

Understanding the Basics of the ANS (Autonomic Nervous System): Body

The ANS is truly the super intelligence of the human body, and it is regulated by the Hypothalamus of the Limbic System in the brain, operating continually and unconsciously, keeping us balanced and in good health 24/7 (homeostasis).

Unconsciously means that whether we are aware of it or not, all vital functions of our bodies are constantly kept operational without us having to consciously or voluntarily intend it to do so. Our bodies are regulated, controlled, and balanced for us each moment, naturally and organically, by the Involuntary Actions of the ANS. Examples of Involuntary Actions are:

- the functioning of our vital organs
- the beating of our heart
- breathing/respiration
- vasomotor activity
- reflex actions such as sneezing, coughing, swallowing, and vomiting
- digestion
- pupillary response
- urination
- sexual response

The ANS is a very important part of the trauma experience. It is divided into two parts: the Sympathetic Nervous System and the Parasympathetic Nervous System. The Sympathetic Nervous System is considered the "fight or flight" system, while the Parasympathetic Nervous System is considered the calm, relaxed, focused system, often referred to as the "rest and digest" or the "feed and breed" system. So we can see that these two systems within the ANS have opposite actions. One activates a physiological response while the other inhibits it. *You cannot be both at the same time.* Either you are "sympathetic" and in "fight or flight" mode, or you are in "parasympathetic" mode, relaxed and calm. Why do we need to understand this, and how does this relate to PTSD?

When a trauma survivor develops PTSD, one of the most frightening and uncontrollable symptoms is known as "triggering". The easiest way to recognize triggering is that one can move extremely quickly into Sympathetic "fight or flight" mode by something nobody else around perceives as danger, but which evokes a traumatic memory for the trauma survivor. It can be simply evoked by a color, a smell, an action, or a sound, causing the triggering of a past traumatic event memory. When you have PTSD there is no way to control this because the Limbic System is already irritated and overreactive, stuck in "fight or flight" and, as a result, not functioning correctly. There is no longer a correct balance between the Intelligent Brain (NeoCortex) and the Emotional Brain (Limbic System), emotions are dominant, and misinformation or partially correct information is being sent to the Frontal Lobe of the brain from a dysfunctional Amygdala and Hippocampus within the Limbic System for clear, logical reasoning. Once triggered, a survivor can be thrown immediately into any one or more symptoms mentioned above. This is a mess, to say the least! And it is extremely frightening for witnesses, friends, and loved ones who typically do not have the knowledge, tools, techniques or understanding to assist the survivor relax and calm down.

The following are two good examples of trauma survivor "triggering":

A rape survivor goes for a relaxing massage. In the normal process of the massage, the masseuse may inadvertently touch an area of the body that causes the client to trigger and "freak out" hysterically or go into a freeze mode, becoming rigid and unfeeling. Both reactions would seem very odd and unreasonable in such a calm, relaxing environment while experiencing a regular, draped, professional massage. If the massage therapist did not do a proper intake by asking whether a client has had trauma in the past, these responses would startle and frighten both the masseuse, who did nothing inappropriate, and the client, who would not expect to have such an extreme reaction of memory triggering from what should have been a good, highly beneficial, therapeutic treatment.

A military veteran with PTSD goes to the grocery store to shop. This is clearly not a war zone, but somebody drops a heavy box and this sound immediately triggers the veteran into a war zone mode. Now triggered to past memories of the sounds of war by the loud bang of the dropped box, this survivor goes into full "fight or flight". With war veterans at this point, anything can happen. People in the store looking at somebody this reactive naturally think he or she is crazy because the store is so far from

Cracking the PTSD Code! The Positive Effects of Trauma Touch Healing

anything war-like or chaotic. Crazy? Well, yes and no. They just appear to be crazy to those who do not really understand the disorder and how it manifests.

I have proven over the years that *PTSD is absolutely a reversible disorder* if we follow the very specific, organic method I will explain later in the chapter. The *effect* of using the Trauma Touch Healing method gently releases the "fight or flight" electrical charges through channels and systems already established in the body—i.e., we are already pre-wired to cope with trauma to receive, react, and release, naturally. Practitioners merely need to learn this simple, unique method to induce a release of the unwanted, accumulated trauma and pressure building inside. In cases where trauma has caused the brain to become stuck in "fight or flight" and this person is habitually and unconsciously holding onto negative emotions caused by the trauma experience(s), then intervention is necessary, and we must assist by stepping in and *inducing* a release. When trauma is released from the body using a natural method, then *all* systems related to trauma are cleared out, and the body very quickly returns to normalcy, health, and happiness.

When our highly sensitive neurological systems have become dysfunctional, and our emotions have become so far out of balance and dominant, it naturally evokes very unbalanced, overreactive responses. Over time this becomes highly destructive, not only to the survivor themselves, but it also has a negative impact on work, colleagues, family, friends, and worst of all, it systematically undermines and destroys the very loving relationships and partnerships a survivor needs the most. It really behooves us, on every ethical level, to investigate and focus on any and all positive solutions to this hideous condition! Right now, *all* options are *not* being considered, much to the detriment of trauma victims, and survivors.

Well, so far we have connected a PTSD syndrome/pattern/cycle of the Limbic System to the CNS, the PNS, and the ANS. Hopefully it is becoming obvious at this point that we are looking at a much larger group of connecting systems involving PTSD than merely the Limbic System of the brain. Moving forward, there is also another very large system in place that benefits enormously in the clearing out of heavy, negative emotions, which I will explain next.

Understanding the Basics of the Five-layer Energy Body System: Spirit

Without a doubt the fact that we have made such poor progress in the resolution of PTSD within modern mainstream medicine and psychology is the result of incorrect application caused by a definite lack of clear understanding of the healing paradigm: Body, Mind, Spirit. If you think that resolving this highly complex condition can be achieved by treating the physical body, you would be wrong. If you think that a psychologist or psychiatrist focusing on the just the mind will bring resolution, you would also be wrong. If you think that using the Body/Mind paradigm in combination will bring resolution, again you would be wrong.

Why? Because first and foremost we are energetic beings. The entire physical human body is fed energy from the five-layer Energy Body System through a connection point: the neurological system within the physical body. In reality, we have five Bodies: Spiritual Energy Body, Mental Energy Body, Emotional Energy Body, Etheric or Astral Energy Body, and the Physical Energy Body. Humans are created using the Body, Mind, Spirit paradigm, so no *root cause* healing takes place without considering and understanding this concept. Without it, we are merely *symptomatically treating*, not *holistically healing*. And since PTSD impacts the neurological system the most, in order to reverse it, we have no choice but to heal it using the Body, Mind, Spirit paradigm. Logically, nothing else will be or can be successful.

When energy is channeled individually from the Creative Universal Energy Force, the last in line to receive it is the physical body. Depending on which body we require (which depends on our karma and which dimension we appropriately need to be experiencing life), then it is *that* body that needs this energy source to function. Since we reside on Earth in a third-dimensional body (physical body), this is where we will be required to focus primarily. The following information will give you a better understanding of energy. Logically, if the brain and the neurological systems are so involved in trauma and PTSD, as we have already explained, how can we possibly omit an understanding of energy if energy travels throughout our physical bodies directly through our electrical Nervous Systems giving us life? When the Nervous System shuts off the electricity for whatever reason, we are no longer able to sustain life on the physical plane, we experience death, and the physical body becomes useless to us at that point.

Trauma affects not only the Physical Energy Body but also greatly impacts the other energy Bodies as well, because they are all closely inter-connected. The attached higher dimensional Bodies are more pure, subtle and much more sensitive than the physical one, and they can be seen by some as auras around our bodies. When we experience traumatic events or shocks, each of the five Bodies also feels the dramatic effects, and if the negative charges and emotions are not properly released, then pockets of energetic blockages develop in the these subtle energy fields. Blocked energy creates blockages of energy flow, and this subsequently causes problems to the trillions of cells in our physical Body which needs this energy to exist, and function. Trauma impacts the energetic Bodies enormously. Therefore, the paradigm that is successful in healing from traumatic events and PTSD, is releasing the stored/stuck trauma from *all* five Bodies using the Body, Mind, Spirit paradigm.

Logically then, we also need to understand what "spirit" energy really is. Our entire electrical/energetic system is fascinating to study and understand. The universe is alive with atoms vibrating at different speeds of frequency, providing life and power to all living things. With just a basic understanding of the Body, Mind, Spirit paradigm, so many illnesses and dis-eases would get cured in our world! Merely working with the physical body, or just the mind, or even a combination of both is not nearly enough coverage. If we envision a pyramid cut into five equal, horizontally parallel lines, we see that the Spiritual Energy Body at the bottom of the pyramid covers quite a vast area, whereas the Physical Energy Body (triangle) at the top is the smallest area. If we only focused on this small triangle at the top of the pyramid in comparison to the rest of it, we'll get an inkling of how much area is lost in the healing processes within modern mainstream medicine today. When it comes to healing from trauma, the entire pyramid definitely must be considered, and negativity must be released from all energetic bodies to be really effective.

So why can't we see these energy bodies? Because we are not designed to. When in the physical body, we are here to focus on this life, in this dimension. It would be way too distracting and confusing to be experiencing our other bodies simultaneously. While in the physical body our senses are very limited, so we only see the physical and nothing else. However, just outside our line of perception, the other bodies do exist and can be seen. The physical body is the most dense form of energy with a frequency low enough to be seen by our physical eyes within the spectrum of visible light; heard with our ears (with a range of about 30 to 15,000 Hertz); and experienced with the senses such as touch, taste, and smell within the "frequency capability" of our physical body only. There are some people that are capable of experiencing more, but this is not common.

The five-layer Energy Body System is a simplified way of describing the Human Energy Field. While in the physical body, the unseen higher subtle energy bodies overlap and interpenetrate with the lower subtle bodies, which includes the physical body. It is important to note that each of the five bodies is identified by a different frequency (the physical body being the lowest frequency and the spiritual body being the highest). Because all five energy bodies are energetically connected and interwoven with each other, all are affected by what happens to us in the physical body. Likewise, when healing energy is directed to the physical body, it also positively affects the higher energy bodies with healing energy.

When releasing negative energies from the physical body, the recipient of the directed healing energy actually *feels* the release through the sensory nerves of the PNS. The heavy, negative energies leaving the body are often perceived or felt as thick mud, slow-moving lava, or a liquid of honey consistency; newer negative energies being released are felt as a lighter, quicker liquid substance leaving the body. If trauma is only a physical experience, how can this be? Obviously, these perceptions are not physical (no real physical mud or lava is releasing from the body), but they are being sensually experienced as such, so we must come to the logical conclusion that something other than just the physical is at play. Over the years, as I have charted the release sequences while working with clients, I have noticed that the physical body releases unwanted negative energy through the CNS (head and spine), PNS (especially hands and feet), and through the energetic Meridian Lines, directed (exactly of *where* to work) by the Autonomic Nervous System. The ANS, as a constant, unconscious super intelligence of the body utilizes all bodily systems at its disposal to dispel and discharge what it does not need in its attempts to maintain homeostasis. So, while we have previously discussed the systems of the CNS, PNS, ANS and the five-layer Energy Body System, we also need to explain what the Meridian Lines are, as they represent an entirely different energy flow system within the body.

Understanding the Basics of the Meridian Lines: Spirit

The Meridian Lines make up an energetic system within our physical body. They are invisible to the human eye, but without them we could not sustain life. In a similar way that blood is carried throughout the body by arteries, meridians carry energy. They are our body's "energy bloodstream" bringing vitality and balance together with the capability of removing energy blockages, stagnations and imbalances, adjusting metabolism, and determining the speed and form of cellular change. Their natural, unobstructed flow is as critical to us as the flow of blood, affecting all the major systems of the body. In traditional Chinese medicine, this system of pathways through which life-energy flows is known as Qi (chee), and they have been mapped throughout the body over thousands of years by acupuncturists. Meridians exist in corresponding pairs, and each meridian has many acupuncture points along its path.

There are twelve major Meridians, each relating to a specific organ or part of the body, and in Chinese medicine these natural energy pathways are used for healing. If a Meridian energy pathway becomes obstructed or unregulated then a clear flow of energy cannot move as it should, often causing physical problems in our bodies. So again we see that "heavy" unreleased trauma (this time in the energy channels) can create energy blockages, and if these blockages are left untreated, they often cause problems to our health one way or another. Sometimes serious, life-threatening health issues can result.

So if we visit the acupuncturist, will this reverse the condition of PTSD? No, it will not. The reason is that the Meridians are just *one* part of the Body, Mind, Spirit paradigm, not the totality. It is just one system among many other systems in the body that is affected by traumatic events. When you see a physician regarding trauma, he or she will attempt to treat the physical body. If there is any physical damage, physicians will use their knowledge and skills to correct this. They may then refer you to a psychologist if emotional issues develop, and while this is an excellent next step treatment for three to six months, if a trauma survivor stays indefinitely in psychotherapy, usually things start to go awry. The longer a survivor stays in psychotherapy and is not referred to the next crucial step of discharging the stored/stuck energy, the longer the trauma remains in the body, building up tremendous pressure in the ANS over time, and filtering more deeply into the trillions of cells and tissues of the body. In addition, negative energy, if not released, causes unhealthy energy blockages in the meridians. These blockages, if also left untreated, will cause imbalances in the body, which over time begins to overwhelm the immune system, resulting in the development of diseases and illnesses. We cannot "talk out" trauma.

PTSD results from the ANS not discharging stored energy from trauma, and thus preventing the system from resetting itself.

So, in order for a trauma survivor to regain good health and balance, we must intervene and induce the release of stuck energy and built-up pressure in the nervous system, as well as eliminate the heavy, negative energy blockages in the meridians. It is very unfortunate that, in general, mainstream medicine chooses to understand only the physical aspects of the body (the Body/Mind paradigm), and within their respective healing modalities completely ignores and disregards the true energetic nature and essence of what creates *all* life, keeping every single cell in the physical body alive and healthy. How can we ignore the very basics of life (pure energy/spirit) in any equation of healing? It is a stunning and tragic omission!

If you do not educate yourself about the building blocks of life at the quantum level, and you do not understand energy's basic nature, then what can you really understand about the complex processes of trauma which slams out of left field into our physiological, mental, neurological, and energetic systems, running amuck if not released and controlled, and creating chaos and destruction in all the body's systems? How can you possibly come to the proper healing solutions from such a level of ignorance? When you look at how the most important part of the equation (spirit) is ignored (often intentionally and stubbornly by traditional medicine) and therefore clearly not understood, how can you realistically help anybody with PTSD? It shouldn't come as any surprise then to hear about all the horrendous solutions doctors, researches, and everybody in between, have come up with to treat PTSD. Additionally, little bits and pieces of treatment will not achieve a reversal of this condition, simply because of the extreme complexity and interconnectedness of PTSD. This condition needs a very focused, comprehensive, knowledgeable, and balanced treatment plan if there is any hope of reversal. I'm happy to tell you that the solution is simpler and easier than anybody would have guessed or imagined! And the exquisite beauty of the solution is that it's natural, and organic. This is what Trauma Touch Healing (TTH) offers.

Understanding the Natural Solution to Reverse PTSD: The ANS Method

When we experience a trauma, the sensory nerves of the PNS receive the incoming information and carry it to the CNS, where the brain jumps into action to preserve life. We have also discussed how a severe trauma or repeated traumas can cause the neurological systems to either shut down or stay frozen open in the "flight or fight" mode. Over time, repeated traumas and daily triggering (also causing a flight-or-fight response) which do not release but instead remain held in the body, filters ever more deeply into each cell of the body (causing cell dysfunction and *dis*-eases). Lately, the results of research on PTSD even suggest that trauma embeds itself into our DNA!

If trauma is severe enough, or sustained enough, and these constant, powerful fight-or-flight electrical charges remain unreleased, then *pressure* builds up in the body. This causes dysfunction and imbalances in every system, including cells and tissues, and must eventually be released to regain good health, balance, and sanity in order to thrive again. So how is this achieved? How do we release it? Simple…once again we must turn to the sensory nerves. This is where the trauma entered our system, and this is where it will also be released. But how exactly is this done?

Remember, we possess a body that is already wired to cope with the intake and release of trauma. We only have to watch animals to see this release taking place after trauma: the trembling of muscles as trauma releases, possibly some purging (such as urination, defecation, vomiting), and then after a little time the animal regains its balance and moves on. The unfortunate response of humans with intelligence is that we tend to over-analyze, think too much, feel too much, and seem to love holding onto deep hurtful or negative emotions instead of simply letting them go. So when a Trauma Touch Healer is presented with somebody suffering from PTSD, we slowly and carefully induce energetic releases over a period of three months. This process of reversal *must* be done very carefully and slowly to keep a client safe and balanced during the process in order to avoid purging and any extreme reactions.

I always imagine a client as a delicate silk cloth caught on a thorn bush. In order to prevent any tearing of the cloth, the extrication of the cloth from the thorns must be done with gentle, surgical precision. Perhaps now you can understand how those treating clients with PTSD without a deep knowledge of the subject merely end up, in their ignorance, damaging clients even more by re-traumatizing and re-victimizing them if the therapy sessions are done too fast, or without an awareness of triggering, dissociation, and so on, or even worse, not knowing how to control these responses.

Once again, how do we induce a *real* emotional and pressure release? The easiest way is to connect with a client's sensory nervous system. How do we do this? We do this by asking the client to feel sensations in the body. Sensations are innocuous and non-threatening, and feeling them doesn't emotionally shut down a client which is usually what happens when asking them to connect with their feelings or emotions. The five traditional senses of the Sensory System are: sight, smell, touch, taste and hearing. However, there are a myriad of other much more subtle senses that are utilized by the ANS to direct where therapists should work with their hands. The ANS constantly "talks" (communicates) with us through these subtle sensations.

Remember: PTSD is the result of the ANS not discharging stored energy from trauma, and thus preventing the system from resetting itself.

The ANS, being the energetic super-intelligence of the body, controls and aids everything in the body to maintain life, health, and homeostasis. It also knows everything that has happened in that body, as well as how to remedy it in order to maintain balance and good health again. Under certain traumatic circumstances the body can become overwhelmed, and this often negatively impacts many systems within the body as we have previously discussed. This is especially true of PTSD, so therapists are compelled to intervene in assisting clients to rid themselves of stored electrical charges from trauma, as well as releasing the intense pressure continuously building up inside. The trick, as a therapist, is knowing *how* to make contact with the ANS. The answer is through sensations, provided to both the client and therapist from the ANS.

When we ask a client to feel a dominant sensation in the body in order to begin the trauma release work, it quickly becomes quite evident that the Autonomic Nervous System has its own unique way of guiding both client and therapist on the correct pathway, using very specific sequences and patterns to reverse the trauma from the body. The ANS, in its wisdom, always utilizes the best and gentlest way to unwind trauma, very similar to peeling an onion. As a super-intelligence, the ANS is fully capable of using the purest energy and utilizing the best knowledge available, as it is already aware of all the information and patterns of exactly how the traumas became entrenched in a particular body. Therefore, it also already knows the *solution* of how to reverse these patterns in the *correct* sequence. Using intuition alone does not release trauma in the correct sequence for reversal, plus using *only* intuition when working on healing a trauma survivor is very unreliable and harmful, since nobody has reached spiritual perfection, and therefore all of us are automatically intuitively suspect.

As therapists all we have to do is teach our clients to feel the sensations fed to it from the ANS, and then induce releases by touching the very specific sensation areas the body provides us. It is very important to keep the client safe and "present" so they do not lose focus and dissociate during the session.

It is an extraordinary process to witness, and over a three month period one can only watch in wonder at the fast, self-healing powers of body, mind, and spirit at work when given a chance to finally release in a safe environment. When given the opportunity, the body very quickly relieves itself of heavy negative emotions, pressures, and unreleased electrical charges buried deep inside the body.

Understanding the Effects of Working with Sensations: The Benefits

It is the effects of Trauma Touch Healing that are the most extraordinary! It must be said at this point that this is not easy work, and absolutely requires a very particular mind-set in order to do it well, and do it correctly. When allowing the ANS to do its directive work, the therapist must know how to set aside their own ego. There must be a very solid understanding of the body, mind, spirit process so that the therapist has no qualms about stepping aside and allowing the client's body to do exactly what it needs to, without any ego interference. What absolutely interferes with this work is the therapist thinking he or she is doing the work. This is not true. It is the body's ANS directing *where* to work from within, and pure universal energy assists the ANS by flowing *through* the therapist from without. The therapist merely becomes a conduit. That is how PTSD gets properly reversed out.

This is a very different but necessary approach for most therapists, especially for "energy workers." That's why most therapeutic, medical, and mental solutions for PTSD so widely miss the mark. Energy workers, especially, can be very egotistical because they think very few people know how to work with energy (so they feel special), and they also falsely believe that their limited intuition is accurate enough for them to figure out the correct healing solutions. Usually they will place their attention on the "issue" areas, but this is not how the ANS works at all. Ditto for psychologists who think they are the mental solution to PTSD, and another ditto for neurologists who seem to come up with the worst and most damaging solutions of all. Symptomatic treating brings very little success to the condition of PTSD. What is required is a full, systemic treatment plan that well understands the full range of complexities associated with the effects of trauma, and a therapist willing to let the body direct the treatment.

To energy bodyworkers I will say this: The problem of PTSD is so complex and so widespread within the various systems of a body that working *only* with imperfect human intuition (a rock being "0" and Creator being "100"), will never assist a client needing serious help, no matter how well-meaning one is. It is only when one learns to surrender to the greater powers that already exist (Creator and ANS both operating on pure energy at the highest level), that one becomes capable of allowing stuck energy to release in the correct way, and especially in the correct sequence. Energy workers should also be educated on how to keep a client safe by knowing how to prevent dissociation and re-traumatization during the therapeutic release process. When you *allow* pure energy to work and flow *through* you, success is achieved!

According to Universal Law, as a therapist in any energetic healing capacity you are nothing (you are merely a tool), but you are also everything (because without you the work cannot be done). It is a metaphysical conundrum or dichotomy of understanding for sure, but If you can achieve and grasp the concept of this essential mind-set, as well as learn the various techniques, here are some of the *beneficial effects* of Trauma Touch Healing that your clients will achieve and enjoy:

1. As pressure is slowly released week after week, episodes of expressed negative emotions from triggering begin to subside, become less and less frequent, and a calmness begins to take over.

2. During sessions special breathing techniques are shown and taught to bring somebody parasympathetic from sympathetic (triggering). This effect is confidence- building. When clients realize that there is something they can actually do to control triggering and re-traumatization (instead of being controlled by it), it's the first step to empowerment that was initially ripped away by the traumatic event(s).

3. As the body empties trauma from the cells and tissues, it becomes and feels lighter (this sensation occurs when the heavy emotional blockages get progressively released and removed). Quite quickly a natural happiness and joy automatically replaces the heavy, sad, depressive feelings from before.

4. Boundaries are re-established in one special session in an experiential way, so that clients feel and fully understand that they hold the power to allow or disallow somebody into their personal space. They learn that they hold the power to decide and discern who enters and interacts with them in a personal way or not. This is a huge step

forward, particularly for victims of abuse on all levels (especially rape victims). Research has found that a loss of boundaries is one of the first casualties of all traumatic experiences.

5. As pressure is released from the neurological systems, the positive effect on the Limbic System is quite dramatic. Clients perceive that they can now more easily focus and concentrate, and thoughts that had felt "cloudy" and "muddled" before become clearer as the Frontal Lobes begin to re-set and become more organized for clear, logical reasoning (i.e. the Working Memory is restored). Because of the plasticity of the brain, as pressure is released from the ANS, it quickly reorganizes itself and the normal, natural balance between the Limbic System and the NeoCortex is restored. Suddenly a client begins to feel like a well-functioning, balanced human being, adding to that individual's confidence and empowerment. When done correctly, this process is achieved extraordinarily fast, and normally a client is already feeling these positive changes well before the three months of treatments is completed.

6. An interesting effect to observe is the large vibrational shift in a client. As the heavy emotional charges are being "let go" and as clients begin to experience and explore their "new" lightness, perceptions of themselves and their environment also begin to shift. It becomes obvious how they are feeling when (usually halfway through treatment) clients present themselves in completely different clothes. It is not uncommon for a client, now no longer feeling victim to the heavy, depressive emotional "old" self, to literally throw out their entire wardrobe of clothes to buy new, fresh clothes reflecting their "new" self. They usually select light-colored, colorful clothing. It is delightful to observe this positive change when clients begin to see themselves as healthy and happy, instead of relating to themselves as being a victim.

7. As the Trauma Touch Healing therapy continues, the brain, normally stuck in an "old" pattern of very limited black-or-white choices (a classic symptom of PTSD), begins to loosen as the old patterns start to break down, and this is replaced by a new pattern where choices open up in a much more horizontal way. As the brain is given the opportunity to heal from trauma, a new paradigm of multiple

choices unfolds and releases clients of their past limitations. Again, this is a great source of freedom and confidence-building.

8. Quite early into the Trauma Touch Healing therapy, the old "tapes" of the unpleasant trauma memories that repeatedly play in the brain during PTSD (and never seem to shut off) start to fade and disconnect. When the ANS assists in releasing pressure in the Limbic System, with it also goes old, vivid memories of the traumatic events. Clients discover that these "old" memories become what they should be: mere memories. While memories do remain, they feel like very old ones from a long time ago. These organically recede into the past where they belong, and they no longer have the power to affect the present with the usual triggering events so familiar to PTSD sufferers. This is an important step forward for a trauma survivor because the repeated traumatic memories that remain so vivid, ugly, upsetting, and tenacious, are the reason why so many survivors self-medicate in an attempt to prevent memories from surfacing and controlling them. Alcohol and drugs (street and prescription) are usually the medications of choice to numb the brain to maybe get a little sleep or achieve some quality of life. You can only imagine the relief a PTSD client feels when they discover that these awful memories start fading by themselves as Trauma Touch Healing therapy proceeds, and real healing takes place! This too is a joy to witness.

9. One of the most interesting effects of using the method of sensations, is that a client will actually feel the stuck/stored emotions and energy leaving the body through the various systems. They describe how it feels: At the beginning, the old "stuff" is felt as thick mud or lava slowly leaving the body. Usually these old, heavy emotions will leave via the fingers and toes. Let's say the ANS has directed the client and therapist to the shoulder area. As the therapist works on this area, movement will be felt under the therapists hands, and then the client will report that the heaviness is moving down the arms into their hands and out through their fingers as it releases. Sometimes this mud or lava is so thick that it has a tendency to stick in the joints and can cause mild pain which lets the therapist know to unblock this area so the heaviness can proceed and exit. While this is one feeling

of release, there are others: a dissolving sensation into the therapists hands, a feeling that steam is releasing from the issue area into the therapist's hands, or tingling sensations are felt in hands and feet as energy releases. While these are common experiences, clients will be able to clearly describe many other sensations. They will also easily be able to describe *what* is trapped in an issue area such as the size, color, shape, and material it is made of. Particularly stubborn areas perceived by the client may be made of metal (steel), which invites more sophisticated methods of removal. An experienced therapist learns that the smaller and more compact the target for removal - especially if its color is black - the greater its impact will be on the client when releasing. Often these areas will cause dissociation during a release if not quickly intercepted. Pathways observed during a particular session while releasing vary, but clearly the ANS uses all systems available. Releases are observed processing through the PNS, often the large Meridians, as well as the CNS, particularly when releasing out of the top of the head. From this you can see that when working with trauma releasing, a therapist needs to be not only very knowledgeable on the subject, but also well-trained. This is not work for those who simply like the idea of helping PTSD sufferers. If you want to really assist traumatized clients, please get the proper training!

10. Very quickly after starting therapy, a very interesting effect happens to clients regarding personal relationships, especially those close to them. They literally come out of the "ether" let's say. Since like attracts like, most PTSD sufferers are attracted to other PTSD sufferers (you can see why relationships fail to flourish when both parties have the condition). However, when one is releasing while the other is not, the one engaged in therapy starts to observe quite easily how the partner or friend is exhibiting symptoms of PTSD never noticed before. The more release work clients do, the more they are able to see and perceive how others are trapped in the cycle of PTSD, and they begin to be uncomfortable with it. It is always best when working with couples that *both* complete the therapy. However, since the process can be quite strenuous at the beginning, it is recommended that one starts therapy first, followed by the other when the first client is halfway through theirs. Remember, like attracts like. The

healed person usually moves on to seek the company and compatibility of more emotionally healthy and stable people, as they should.

The goal of TTH is to *permanently* reverse and release trauma out of the body by the method of sensations to achieve the positive effects mentioned above, and much more!

Testimonials

Before TTH therapy begins, clients are asked what they would like to *achieve* from the therapy. When the full course of therapy is completed, they are asked again what they feel they *gained* from the therapy. Below are a few of these "before and after" comments from clients who have completed the treatment. Please remember that each "after" comment comes after only three months of work! The processing continues as the neurological systems continue to heal, with the most dramatic positive changes observed occurring two years after the completion of therapy! The following excerpts were provided by the clients, and are presented verbatim:

Before: I want to feel better about myself and be released from suppressed feelings of guilt.

After: I feel as if a great weight has been lifted and I feel like a clear, empty crystal glass. Thank you for realigning my energy and clearing the mess from my body. *Former Navy SEAL*

Before: I want to experience more sensation and feeling in my body and connect to it.

After: I feel very light and carefree. I feel humbled by the fact that I can now organize/interpret every scenario that comes my way. Being more in-tune with my senses has allowed me certain beneficial changes in my life. The people, posture, and even how people perceive me have all changed for the better. Thank you! *University student*

Before: I want to come to terms and handle negative situations in a positive way and affect those around me with this knowledge in a new positive way.

After: I feel so exhilarated, happy, and have a clear mind. I hope I will be able, in a small way, to share my happiness and install it in my family. I also feel quite able to cope and turn around any negativity that comes my way. These past weeks have proved to me that the therapy is priceless, and if I can share a fraction of what you have taught and given, I will be one of the happiest people alive. Thank you. *CEO/Owner of large company*

Before: I want to relieve stress, become more self-aware and less dissociative.

After: I feel better than when I started TTH. I see the difference and feel less fearful and more open. Working with you has been amazing and I would recommend this therapy to anyone who feels like they need this. *Massage therapist*

Before: I want to acquire tools and skills to better carry on with my family.

After: I feel energized and happy. I appreciated your flexibility and free allowance/acceptance of me expressing my power. *Engineer*

Before: I want to be as healthy as possible while in action and to fulfill my dreams coming to fruition. I want to release trauma and fear. I want new confidence, full power, and I want to feel safe!

After: I feel beautiful and powerful. I feel totally tapped into joy, peace, vitality! Trauma Touch Healing has completely empowered me and altered the happiness in my life for the better. *Professional Singer*

Before: I want not to be angry. If want to be able to take back myself when in an argument. Stop shutting down and be able to build lasting relationships.

After: I feel lighter and balanced. My body feels clear. I feel absolutely wonderful. Trauma Touch Healing was the best thing ever. I feel amazing. I got my life back. Thank you. *Security Guard/Ex-Military*

Before: I want to resolve past trauma and become healthier.

After: I feel really confident with my new skills of being in touch with my body and what I need to do. I am excited about all the new information I have and how perfectly everything is releasing. I'm really excited! *Masseuse*

Before: I want to overcome this "stuck" feeling.

After: Trauma Touch Healing is a great program! Lots of changes and transformation (have happened). Thanks! *Project Manager*

Before: I want no pain.

After: I feel a powerful peacefulness, higher clarity. Keep doing what you are doing as you change people's lives. Thank you. *Hotel Manager*

Before: Really, I am tired of living in a way where I feel like I have not been able to achieve many of the goals I have for myself. I want to feel like I am in control of my life.

After: Trauma Touch Healing has allowed me to think that things are moving now in a wonderful direction. This is what it could be. I think it has been a completely amazing journey. Things are so possible now! *Therapist and Marathon Cyclist*

The above testimonials are just a few examples of the results and effects of release work using Trauma Touch Healing methods. Looking around at the world today, it is with great sadness that I observe the enormous amount of people who are traumatized each and every day without any really good solutions emanating from mainstream medicine. It pains me deeply to look at the global suffering when therapeutically I achieve so much success in this area using safe, natural methods. The Trauma Touch Healing method should be globally known!

Please spread the word to those around you who are depressed and disillusioned and still hungering for a good, successful, safe, permanent, drug-free, organic solution to their PTSD suffering. Most of all, I would like survivors to know that they should never give up, and that with work and effort after a traumatic experience, there absolutely is a successful pathway to freedom, empowerment, thriving, and happiness again!

Survive to Thrive!

SIX

What Is Dissociation?

One of the great secrets of trauma healing is realizing and becoming aware of dissociation. Most clients I have treated have no idea they do it. They have done it for so long that it has become second nature, and they dissociate unconsciously. So what is dissociation? Dissociation is a mental checking out, splitting off, spacing out, or numbing out that a trauma victim does to emotionally survive the trauma or a survivor does when trauma memory is triggered. Initially, this is done to separate oneself from the horror of the trauma. It is instinctual—a survival tool we have at our disposal when the trauma being experienced becomes too overwhelming and unbearable, and we can no longer tolerate the brutality of it emotionally. The problem with dissociation is that when dissociated, you are not *present* in the moment. You have been triggered and have now spontaneously shifted into the *past*.

Initially, it feels good to dissociate and cut oneself off from the intensity of the trauma experience. Numbing and dissociating feel far better than feeling and enduring the dreadful, raw negative emotions. The problem comes in when this checking out or numbing out becomes habitual every time there is a trigger. Triggering occurs when anything happens in our day that forces us to remember the trauma or associates us with a past trauma experience. It simultaneously causes a return of the awful, old emotional feelings. Trauma survivors usually immediately check out to the safety zone of dissociation.

Once we are caught in the trauma vortex and frozen in the cycle of PTSD, being triggered becomes a daily occurrence anytime we encounter stressors. In a hyperaroused state, which already keeps the body in a highly sympathetic, stressed state, always ready to fight or flee, any added stress of daily life become overwhelming. A survivor will find himself automatically going to that place of safety, numbness, and distance where he cannot be reached to feel any negative emotions. But as mentioned before, when numb, we cannot feel any positive emotions either! Numbing is not selective; we are either connected or disconnected to our emotions.

Often victims of trauma will spontaneously leave their bodies and watch the trauma as it unfolds, standing in spirit somewhere nearby split off from themselves. We hear this often in cases of rape or near-death experiences. Like millions of others, I learned to do this as a child when I needed to escape to a better mental and emotional place than what was being experienced in my home life.

So if it feels so good and safe, what is the problem experiencing it? Here is the problem: As explained above, when a survivor is dissociating, he/she is not present. A survivor is either in one place or the other. You cannot be present and dissociative at the same time, and this can become detrimental. Why is dissociating detrimental? I will give a few examples of why, when no longer engaged in the actual trauma, uncontrollable dissociating is not a benefit anymore.

Example 1

I had learned dissociation so well as a child that as an adult, one of my dreadful habits, when driving long distances in the car, was to completely dissociate while driving. I could drive a distance of fifty miles or more and have absolutely no recollection of how I got from point A to point B. None. I could mentally split off from the person driving (me) and go completely into another world of thought, thinking and sorting out many things in my mind but completely unconscious to what I was actually doing. When I would gain consciousness and look around, I would notice I was always driving at the correct speed limit and the correct distance behind the car in front of me. However, I would have no memory at all of how I got there. Interestingly enough, I always seemed to become present before I needed to turn off the freeway. I am sure all reading this would agree that it does not sound like a healthy way to drive! I am happy to say that since undergoing Trauma Touch Healing, I no longer do this.

Example 2

I had a young client who was a student studying at university. He suffered from PTSD due to childhood trauma, and one of his adult symptoms was procrastination. So, of course, when there were school projects due during midterms or finals, he would put them off till the last moment and then have one or two days at best to complete them all! At this point, he would be under so much stress that to escape the stress he had created from procrastination, he would dissociate. As a result, completing his projects became an uphill battle. I surely don't have to point out that this did not serve him well when trying to work on difficult school projects that demanded all his intellectual reasoning! Of all the times he really needed to be present with a clear mind, it was at exam time. Instead, he would spontaneously dissociate in those moments, becoming spacey, ungrounded, and fractured in his thinking. I was personally thrilled that after completing therapy with me, he gained control of both procrastination and dissociation and was able to complete his studies and earn his degree very successfully.

Example 3

We hear time and time again about people going into rages, blacking out and not being present, and then killing somebody, which they then have no memory of. Very scary. I often wonder how many prisoners and death row inmates have experienced difficult trauma pasts, learned to dissociate, and suffer from PTSD but, due to a lack of accurate diagnosis and correct treatments, end up in the prison system.

Example 4

Imagine being a commanding officer in a war who suffers from PTSD. During the stress of battle, you are triggered and then uncontrollably dissociate, but you still have to give directions to those soldiers under your command. I talked with such an officer one day. He had tears in his eyes from the guilt he feels that perhaps, under these circumstances, he was making erroneous decisions and sending soldiers to their deaths. Very tough. And since it is a professional death sentence for a military personnel to admit that they have PTSD, they are forced to stay silent to keep their jobs.

Example 5

What about athletes who become triggered during the high stress of competitions? If I had known how to control dissociation while on the tennis court, I would have been so much more of an awesome athlete. It is very difficult under the high stress of competing to win if you are not feeling grounded and are not highly focused, no matter how good you are. I see many athletes who would benefit very much from knowing how to do correct breathing, calm down, get present and grounded, and be able to concentrate clearly. This would be an athlete who would be *in the zone* and very difficult to beat!

Example 6

There are bodyworkers who also dissociate while doing bodywork. How can a bodyworker be really effective in their job if they are dissociated? Even bodyworkers need to know the technique to stay present in their bodies to be able to provide their services properly and ethically, to the best of their ability. We all owe this to our clients!

Example 7

What if you had gone through the trauma of a car accident, and after recovery, you now had to get back into the car to drive on roads and freeways? What if you were filled with such anxiety at the prospect of being on the road again and behind the wheel of the car that you began to dissociate? Would you be a good, focused, aware driver on the road? No, you would not. There would be the high possibility that you would create another car accident.

The examples can go on and on. The point of the examples is to show that when we are dissociative and not present in the body, we are not at our best for anything! I often wonder to myself how many people walk around us in dissociative states, performing poorly as they struggle to focus, forcing those around them to also bear the consequences.

It is very important that we learn to recognize the method of how we dissociate (everyone has a different way of doing it), learn how to stop it as we are beginning to enter dissociation, and then learn the method and the feeling of what it's like being *present* in our bodies. This way, we can create a new, positive habit of staying there, and preferably processing emotions while being present. With the correct tools to help you change the old learned mindset, controlling dissociation is absolutely possible. Imagine the empowerment this brings to have dissociation under *your control* at last!

We have talked about this already, but again, when bodyworkers are not educated on dissociation, they will often induce an emotional release during their work but not have the understanding or knowledge to keep you present at the same time. The moment you are having an emotional release while dissociated (back in your past), you are being re-victimized and re-traumatized! You are being hurt, not helped.

What Is Dissociation?

During any somatic emotional release work, it is imperative to be present in your body at the same time and be receiving treatment from a therapist who knows how to achieve this. If you are presently receiving, or contemplating receiving, bodywork treatment for trauma with a therapist who does not know this or cannot clearly explain it to you (refer to the list in Chapter Four), you are not in the best of hands to be specifically treated for trauma or PTSD. This is how important it is!

SEVEN

Re-creating Lost Boundaries

What if each night somebody crept into your bedroom and, without your permission, climbed into your bed and raped you night after night, over and over again whenever they felt like it? Would you learn healthy boundaries this way? If somebody does not respect *your* personal boundaries how, as a child, will you ever learn to respect another persons boundaries ? As a child sexual or emotional or physical or psychological abuse survivor, how would you even know what a healthy boundary actually is? You would not. You could not. Because in each case, there is a total disrespect and willful violation of personal boundaries and personal sacred space by the perpetrator. Children must learn from their elders how to respect the boundaries and personal space of others. So these boundary violations that abuse victims must endure, are not only highly traumatizing, but also very disempowering. What if the perpetrator themselves were child victims of abuse and never learned boundaries? Could they teach their children? Of course not. So re-creating and re-establishing *healthy* boundaries for abuse survivors is essential!

Loss of boundaries, however, is not exclusive to physical, emotional, and sexual abuse survivors. You may have had an abuse-free childhood, let's say, but then experienced a severe shock trauma in adulthood. This event blasts into you like a nuclear bomb, catapulting you so far beyond anything normally experienced in life up to that point, that it also takes you out of the safe, secure box of everything previously known to you—your life's boundaries. The tight walls of the sum total of your life experience up to that poignant, traumatic moment are suddenly and instantly torn open and smashed apart. In the aftermath, you now feel completely lost. Unsafe. Insecure. Who are you? You don't know anymore. You thought you knew, but now this new life-altering experience has blown apart everything you thought you previously knew about yourself and your life. You feel a desperate need to piece it all together again and regain your power and security—your space. It is, therefore, very essential to healing from trauma that you get back your boundaries and structure again. So how do you do this?

I have never treated anybody who has not heard of boundaries and the need to get them back. It is always introduced and talked about by the psychologists in treatment. But I quickly noticed that knowing about boundaries on an intellectual level and feeling a boundary energetically are two very different experiences. When I introduce the subject of boundaries in Trauma Touch Healing (we do one entire session dedicated to this), I usually get the following common response: "Oh, you don't need to teach me that. My psychologist explained it to me over and over again. Trust me, I know all about boundaries." However, when doing an intake, it has never failed that I notice quite quickly that the client in front of me has no real boundary awareness at all. They are wide open. This is very common in trauma survivors and very easy for the therapist to detect. A personal energetic boundary must be understood on an intellectual level but, more importantly, it must also be consciously *felt*.

One repercussion of having no boundaries is an endless number of problems with personal relationships. This is a clue and will show up in the intake, if it is thorough. It's really interesting to detect trauma survivors this way. Often survivors attempt to overcompensate their lack of power by becoming super overachievers, and this often shields them from detection by the average person. I have people tell me, "Oh, so-and-so doesn't suffer from PTSD. Look at his life and how successful he is." But when you look at that person's relationship history, it is often a complete mess.

If you are not in possession of a healthy boundary, healthy relationships are very difficult to have. Like attracts like, and somebody with no boundaries feels far more compatible and comfortable with another person who also has no boundaries. Really, why would somebody with a healthy boundary want to have a relationship with somebody with no boundaries? How successful would this relationship be when one person is constantly and unconsciously plodding and trampling at will in and out of the other's sacred space? It would last two seconds! Imagine the reactions of a person with no boundaries being told they couldn't do something because it was violating the other person's space. How long do you think that relationship would last?

Re-creating Lost Boundaries

A person who is unaware of his boundaries does not like being restricted in any way. He doesn't understand what it means to respect somebody else's space, and he is not used to being contained this way. In the trauma healing world, we see survivors struggling with boundary issues of all kinds and choosing mates/partners with similar struggles. Do I need to tell you how well the relationship of two people with no boundaries is going to go? It isn't. It is just a matter of time before it collapses after vicious fights and abuses of all kinds, while also dragging the unlucky traumatized children who are born into these households with it. Lack of healthy boundaries is a very unhealthy state that affects an entire circle of people around a single survivor.

On the positive side, once a healthy boundary is established again, the survivor will discover that this new energetic change will now attract a person also in possession of a healthy boundary. This has a much better chance of becoming a good, healthy, loving relationship. It will positively affect those people around them and teach the children in this family what a respectful, loving, healthy boundary looks like. Imagine the positive worldwide effect that establishing individual healthy boundaries would have on an entire planet of people!

It is a very easy exercise to have somebody *feel* where her boundary is. We are all in possession of an energy that gives our bodies life and radiates around us. It may often be seen as an aura around the body. It is an electrical energy that sustains us. When it is withdrawn or severed, our bodies are no longer functional. This electrical energy field can be felt as something very tangible when a person is consciously made aware of it. It can expand or contract at will and is also permeable and flexible. When hardened and shielded, it can repel negative energy directed at it. When softened and made flexible and permeable again, it can even allow another energy to enter, if invited. Everybody should be able to have the joy and feeling of empowerment knowing about their own energy field and how to use it. It takes about an hour of special exercises to get a person aware of his boundaries again. Most clients are absolutely amazed at the end of the hour how powerful they feel after being made aware of it. It is a wonderful protection tool to have in one's arsenal.

Once a boundary is firmly established, one can feel a negative energy attempting to invade your space from very far off. The moment they begin to radiate into your aura, you are able to feel and detect them—long before they reach you physically. This is an advantage, especially for those who have suffered abuse and had their energetic boundaries invaded and violated. For these survivors, it feels very strengthening to be able to feel and recognize negative entities or energy coming at them before they're reached and be able to take proactive, preventative measures. In fact, it's very empowering. Personally, I learned how to use my energy field over the years by a combination of spiritual exercises involving meditation, martial arts, and Trauma Touch Healing. Trauma Touch Healing wisely incorporates reestablishing boundaries into the therapy.

There are wonderful benefits to getting our boundaries back. Once a boundary is reestablished and felt (because, in reality, it is always there), besides feeling strong, one also now has a sense of inner security, safety, and organization, which are feelings usually lost to survivors of trauma. Relationships will either shift into healthiness or end as a result of you holding your boundaries and disallowing anybody to invade your space without permission. This important paradigm shift will magnetize more healthy individuals into your life. Likewise, you will learn to respect other's boundaries and learn how not to invade *their* space. Yes, it does work both ways! Once we have our boundaries back and no longer allow others to trample in our energy fields at their will, we also become more sensitive not to violate and disrespect somebody else's space. We become aware of the prior times when *we* have been the invader, and this behavior then becomes uncomfortable and stops. And so, healthy relationships through healthy boundaries, are able to be born and experienced with love, trust, and safety.

Healthy boundaries are flexible and adaptable. When being respected, they allow us to relax. Intimacy and trust can then be developed by allowing us free choice and control of who or what stays out and who or what is invited in to our personal sacred space. This provides us with the opportunity to practice healthy discrimination. This is both empowering, and vitally important to our health!

EIGHT

Finding Joy and Youthful Free Spirit Again!

For a survivor of trauma, the idea of living in a body full of feelings, sensations, memories, and thoughts can be terrifying! And so we sometimes numb ourselves for very long periods of time till eventually we have no feelings, no aliveness, and no joy. We resemble empty shells, unable to enjoy beauty in life or even respond to the touch of a loved one. After meeting survivors of trauma, I have often found that there is a certain heaviness surrounding them—a glumness or heavy depression. They lack a feeling of joy and lightness and laughter. So another secret of trauma recovery is finding joy and the feeling of being a light, free spirit again.

All those years ago in psychotherapy when asked what I wanted, I blurted out, "I want to be free!" To a large extent, this happens naturally when trauma is unloaded and unwound out of body tissue. A great deal of feeling heavy is because the body tissue has become so armored and full and compacted with negative trauma memory that it also begins to feel heavy and stuck to the survivor. Fortunately, it is this sensation in the body that causes a survivor to make the shift in healing to seek a body therapy to help alleviate this feeling. This is the part of trauma healing that cannot be performed by a physician or psychotherapist. The sensation of heaviness and lack of joy is deeply rooted in the emotional body and must be released from there. While a psychotherapist is trained to help emotional problems on the mental level, this training is of no use when attempting to unwind negative emotions out of the body tissue. This somatic negative emotional releasing must be performed by a special trauma-trained bodyworker.

Again, Trauma Touch Healing is a bodywork modality that also addresses the very important process of finding joy in the body through sensation, as well as hands-on bodywork. While using touch to assist the body in releasing the electrical charges held in the cells, at least one session is dedicated to finding one's joy center in the body. What I personally found so empowering about this session is that it gave me the tools to reverse depression very quickly. When a trauma survivor goes into a deep depression, usually caused by triggering, it can sometimes take days to process out of. There is a technique of finding joy in the body using a special process of steps to locate it. Once found, you are able to focus on it and spread it throughout the body with body movements until there is an overall feeling of happiness and joy instead of sadness and depression. The beauty of this is that the process can be done within an hour instead of staying hopelessly stuck in depression for days.

It is a wonderful experience to watch a survivor begin to feel joy again! It is particularly satisfying to see somebody who experienced a childhood full of abuse and who hardly ever got to feel the happiness and lightness of childhood suddenly catch the feeling of joy and youthful free spirit again. To see this survivor begin to shed the heaviness in the release work and then begin to observe and appreciate beauty and feel real happiness is quite an amazing experience for the therapist. It really is like watching the birth of a human as he experiences, sometimes for the first time, the wonder of positive new feelings and sensations. Vitality and a beautiful curiosity of mind emerge from a depressed, numbed out, empty shell of the person that was!

I used to have an office close to the ocean, and sometimes after a session, I would take a walk on the beach with a client. I remember one particular day with a client. We had been working together for about four weeks when we spent a session working on joy, and after this session, we went for a walk on the beach. The client removed his shoes (something he never normally did, he told me) and began to experience the wonderful sensations of the warm sand underfoot. The client remarked how incredible this felt and then became excited about watching the water and the waves crashing onto the shore and how the sun sparkled on the dancing water against the azure blue sky, which was filled with flying seagulls and pelicans. It was like watching a child being taken to the beach for the very first time. Suddenly, this client could really feel and enjoy all the wonderful sensations this magical environment offered. What a joy for me watching him! What a breakthrough! The client was forty-eight years old.

Depression should never be taken lightly. It is a ticking time bomb and a silent killer, often years after the trauma. My aunt was a perfect example of this. She had lost her young son to a drowning incident during a group picnic in a park. He was four years old, and his death was obviously traumatic and shocking. I don't have the benefit of asking her now what treatments she had undergone after the trauma, because she has since passed, but I suspect it was insufficient. About twenty years later, as she washed dishes in her kitchen one day, she looked up to see a neighbor's puppy fall into the swimming pool next door and drown. All the accumulated, unreleased, and unresolved emotional issues from her son's drowning and subsequent triggering over the years erupted into overwhelm, and she experienced a massive neurological breakdown. She took a tailspin into such a deep depression that she had to be hospitalized in a mental institution for many months. She had to undergo intensive treatments to balance herself again. But what if she had just committed suicide? We all know people who seem to be going along in life seemingly just fine, and then one day something happens and they kill themselves. A host of devastated friends and family are left behind, scratching their heads and wondering what went wrong.

Now you know what went wrong—the trauma was never cleared out of the body tissue. It just waits there for years and sometimes decades, further accumulating each time we dissociate and trigger. Finally, it takes just one more powerful trigger to push a survivor over the edge and into the realm of complete overwhelm. When still heavy with trauma and unprepared with techniques to assist during such events, a survivor can very often take no more. That's how essential and important it is for us to learn techniques to help us cope when in need, as well as learn how to clear the heavy, traumatic, negative emotional charges from our body tissues!

It takes bravery and a warrior spirit to wrestle back our lives from the claws and jaws of the mystical dragon, but it is well worth the battle in the end! To be able to move forward in life again, feeling free and light and unstuck while at the same time experiencing power, vitality, and joy—what happiness and what a victory!

NINE

The Emotional Release Process

From the prior chapters, we can begin to see the benefits for trauma survivors of releasing negative emotional charges from our body cells and tissue. In the case of Trauma Touch Healing, the unwinding of the trauma is done in a very unique way. I do believe strongly that this cutting-edge technique will be the future of emotional/energy release work and perhaps integrated into other healing modalities as well.

I have been worked on by a variety of bodyworkers over the years—the physician, chiropractor, physical therapist, acupuncturist, cranial sacral therapist, somatic experiencing therapist, and so-called energy workers of every variety. None of these therapists uses, even remotely, the unique and highly effective techniques of Trauma Touch Healing. One difference is that energy workers usually push and manipulate energy based on their own intuition, but in Trauma Touch Healing, the client's body is given the decision of where to work each time. This is based on the fact that the body will always seek homeostasis (balance and resolution) and also possesses the best knowledge of how the trauma wound into the client's body (which is unique and different in each individual survivor). What better intelligence to appeal to when attempting to unwind and resolve the complications of trauma?

This is why Trauma Touch Healing is so successful, because the *client's body* decides what kind of touch it needs, where to work, and the sequence of areas to be worked on. The client, in essence, heals himself while the therapist, stepping aside of ego and expectation, removes himself from the decision-making and intending process of how to heal the client's body. Instead, the therapist simply reconnects the client to his own body using sensation as a guide. All that needs to be done then is keeping the client safe and present during the emotional release process and controlling the speed of the release.

The body has a fascinating way of letting a client know exactly where it needs resolution and in what order. The client is then taught and encouraged by the therapist how to let it go. This is a very unassuming therapy, and one cannot say at all that the therapist is the one healing the client. It is the client, together with his own body, who is healing himself and finding the resolutions with the guidance of the therapist. This is very empowering to the client. Once this letting go is experienced over and over during therapy sessions, the client then learns the process of releasing trauma himself, becoming proficient at the technique and taking this knowledge away with him when the course of therapy is over. Now you have an educated, enlightened client who, together with all the tools and techniques given to him for dissociation, boundaries, triggering, anger/rage management, and depression, will know exactly how to cope confidently with future trauma-related issues in a safe, correct way. Isn't this so much better than going to therapy and not knowing at all what the therapist just did with you?

I have always argued against and been very nervous of energy workers who claim to do emotional release work but appear to be *doing their own thing*. They will tell you that they use their intuition of where to work on the body to locate energy blocks and clear the body of this negative energy but cannot explain their process. How are we supposed to trust how good and clear the intuition of a healer is? How do you measure this? What about intention? If a bodyworker is using her hands and is therefore in your energy space and she intends anything, this gets injected right into your own energy field, often with negative consequences. Manipulating energy and directing it to various parts of the body is also dangerous, especially if you take into account the fragile states of the body/mind/spirit of a trauma survivor. Manipulating energy into a wrong location or direction or injecting energy into or out of an energy field can have dire consequences to those suffering from any kind of trauma-related issues, especially for somebody suffering with PTSD.

Again, be very careful of whom you have touching your body in an energetic way. Working with and manipulating the body's energy has an extremely powerful effect. If wrongly used or badly applied by a poorly educated energy worker therapist, it can and will harm you. Again, I refer you to Chapter Four and the eleven questions to ask any therapist considering doing energetic emotional release work on you. If the therapist you're considering doesn't have the correct education to work with a trauma survivor, do not have him put his hands on you. If you have already started work with a therapist but are having negative feeling results or the work does not feel like it is doing much to help you, stop and move on. Have the confidence to know your feelings are probably right, because we know our bodies best. Go on to find yourself a more appropriate therapist.

In this chapter, we will do some analyzing of recommended therapies for trauma survivors and how they work. For example, Somatic Experiencing is a modality that also does emotional release work but works very differently than Trauma Touch Healing. It also allows the trauma to release from the body tissue by touch, but to do this, it insists that you go back to the trauma experience in your mind and relive it. I love the fact that Trauma Touch Healing does not require this to release negative emotions. I would not recommend this therapy to any trauma survivor with chronic PTSD and will explain why. Relating to this, I will share two personal experiences regarding Somatic Experiencing—one very negative and one very positive. The following two examples will make it very clear why it is so necessary to be educated about a particular bodywork therapy before receiving treatment.

Example 1

I had traveled to South Africa in the nineties and returned to the United States with a terrible acute pain in my right hip. The pain became so unbearable that I could barely walk and definitely was not sleeping well at night. At first, I thought that it was caused by the horrendously long plane trip there and back. But after two weeks, it was only getting worse. When I focused mentally on this area, I began to get images of the trauma in which my brother died when I had used this right leg and hip to brace myself against the conveyor belt as I frantically tried to pull him free. I began to feel the pain's *root cause* was emotional, not physical. I knew instinctively that I was not going to experience any relief until whatever was in there was released. I also suspected that my trip to South Africa and dealing with my family there had triggered trauma memory that was demanding resolution.

In my mind, I saw that the way to resolve this was with some chiropractic manipulations and heat therapy for the pain, together with some emotional release work. At the time, I was not aware of Trauma Touch Healing however, somebody I knew did Somatic Experiencing, which I understood, in a vague way, helped with emotional releasing from the body.

I first stabilized the hip with chiropractic care and then made my appointment with the Somatic Experiencing therapist. We did a short intake where I relayed my thoughts on which trauma I thought this pain was related to. By then, of course, I was a trauma survivor with chronic PTSD, multiple traumas under my belt, dissociation, and an unhealthy lack of boundaries. But at the time, I didn't know that. I briefly explained the trauma event and explained that I thought most of my trauma during that event stemmed from being left alone afterward. She wrote some notes and proceeded to take me to the therapy room where I was instructed to get onto a massage table and lie down face up. She then covered me with a blanket and switched the main lights out in the room, keeping the room darkly lit with a single low light. This was the first very big mistake for me! I was already nervous and stressed about the release work, and the combination of also being put into darkness caused me to close my eyes. I immediately dissociated from my body. She proceeded to induce emotional releasing.

Earlier I had explained that the worst possible combination for a survivor experiencing emotional release work is to be dissociative at the same time. Even as a very experienced Somatic Experiencing therapist, she was totally oblivious to the fact that I had dissociated. (I know this because she kept asking me where I was.)

Next, I was encouraged to go back to the scene of the trauma. This was a disaster! I literally went through the entire trauma again. Being dissociative at the same time only served to re-traumatize me so severely that by the time the session was completed, I felt ill. I was so emotionally paralyzed that I could not leave her office. Because another client was scheduled, she took me to another empty therapy room, told me to lie on a massage table, covered me with a blanket, switched out the lights, and left me alone in the dark to recover. If you read my trauma experiences well, I think you would immediately know that the issue for me was not only the horrendous shock trauma itself, but the fact that I had been left alone with two drunks afterward (which was like being left with nobody). Back then, alone and in emotional shock, I had fallen into a deep inner dark hole. I was feeling inconsolable pain and anguish and begged for oblivion, which I got when I finally fell into a grateful sleep. I had explained all this to the therapist before the session. But despite this, apparently in complete ignorance, she had just given me the exact same experience all over again! It was really unbelievable.

It took me about three weeks to recover from that single session—not a

The Emotional Release Process

way to go for emotional healing. After I left her office, I got into my car, and my only thought was to get to my chiropractor for some energetic balancing, which he also did. However, I was so traumatized and dissociative after the session and then being left alone in the dark room that I could not drive. So I sat in the parked car outside the office for about another half hour trying to get some kind of focus and equilibrium to drive the thirty-seven miles to the chiropractor's office. I eventually got there somehow. The chiropractor took one look at me, shook his head in disbelief, and asked, "Who did this to you?" Yes, indeed. Beware of therapists who have limited and partial knowledge of trauma!

After this negative experience, I delved more deeply into the technique. Why didn't it work on me? The technique was founded by a man named Peter Levine, who also wrote a book called *Waking the Tiger: Healing Trauma*, which explains the philosophy behind the technique. The therapist who treated me also sold me his book to read regarding the therapy. I did, and it was very interesting. Levine bases his theories on the fact that animals, after being traumatized, will release the traumatic charges from the neurological system almost immediately. This is evidenced by muscle twitching and trembling as the trauma is released after the episode. We humans tend to do the opposite. Our intelligence, unfortunately in these cases, becomes a stumbling block rather than an asset as we prefer to hold onto our emotions and, therefore, onto these negative charges rather than discharging them.

This *holding on* allows the trauma to eventually wind itself deeply into the body tissue. Unless it is let go, it will eventually cause imbalance, diseases, and illnesses. This made sense to me—the letting go of the trauma charges immediately and its obvious value. Of course, in my case, this could not be done, because the trauma was now so old and embedded. By then, I had developed much more complex symptoms of PTSD. The simple "just letting go" of the trauma would never have been enough to help somebody with added issues of fear, anger, depression, lack of boundaries, and dissociation. Looking back, I needed a much more comprehensive therapy at that stage to help me.

Also, the method of visualizing the actual trauma to release it was a huge negative for me. It is so much safer and gentler emotionally to allow the body to release trauma by the use of body sensation to guide the client and therapist. Who wants to go back and visualize the awful trauma event? So triggering! I love this aspect of Trauma Touch Healing, because it becomes completely unnecessary to force a client to go back and view the horror pictures of the past trauma in order to release. But I would, however, also like to give a positive example of Somatic Experiencing.

Example 2

About a year later my one son, who was sixteen years old at the time, was involved in a head-on car collision. Both vehicles were traveling at fifty miles per hour, so you can imagine the impact! The mother and daughter in the SUV, who were not wearing seat belts and both very seriously injured, were airlifted by emergency helicopter to San Diego. My son, who, fortunately, was wearing his seat belt, was not badly hurt, but in the impact he had held onto the steering wheel so tightly that he had bent it and had lost consciousness for a while after the impact. He was taken by ambulance to a hospital where he was examined, X-rayed, and kept under observation for a period of time. When I arrived, the doctor in charge pulled me aside and said that they could find no injuries or broken bones, so they were going to keep him under observation for a little while longer before releasing him. When I approached my son, I wanted to touch his feet for some reason. I looked him over and found he had soreness and bruising on his chest where the seat belt had locked during the impact. Some hematomas were forming on his knees and legs, which we applied ice to in order to stop the inner bleeding. He was also complaining about some neck pain. Interestingly, I kept going toward his feet and wanting to touch and massage them.

He was discharged from the hospital with no further care. Instinctively, I knew he was not right. I knew there was more damage than the medical doctors were aware of. I was right. I immediately took him to a trusted chiropractor who did his own examination and ordered some neck and spine X-rays. He discovered that the cartilage between two of his neck vertebrae had been pushed quite significantly out of alignment during the impact and was quite swollen and aggravated. He immediately started treatment on him. But it was when I had observed my son for a couple of days at home that I noticed he seemed to be a completely different person. He was suddenly very sweet—too sweet. Usually quite outspoken and often caustic-tongued and sarcastic, I suddenly had a different son on my hands. I remembered the Peter Levine book and thought that something had altered emotionally during the impact, and whatever had caused the change, needed to be released from his body as quickly as possible.

I made an appointment with the same Somatic Experiencing therapist who had treated me so disastrously. In this case, however, I thought the treatment was more appropriate. She treated him for a session, and when she was finished, she told me her findings. She said that the impact he had experienced was so severe that his energy field, usually fully encased in the body, had been pushed out with such force that it was still frozen half in and half out of his body. He was completely disorientated, which explained the change in disposition. (This also explained why I had subconsciously and instinctively felt the need to go to his feet initially, to draw his energy back into his body.) She treated him one more time, releasing the shock trauma charges out of the body and assisting him in aligning his energy field back into his body. It took another two weeks before he returned to his former personality and another three months before the neck damage was sufficiently healed. He has no negative aftereffects of this trauma—no PTSD, no neck pains. I believe I had help in finding the correct therapists for him to heal—the physician, the chiropractor, and then the therapist who could release the electrical trauma charges out of the body right away, just like we should do but don't. In this case, I believe that that Somatic Experiencing was a great benefit.

My conclusion is that Somatic Experiencing is just not comprehensive or safe enough to treat the complexities of chronic PTSD but excellent for an immediate release of the negative emotional charges. If we all knew how to release our fight-or-flight charges immediately, just like the animals do, most of us would not develop PTSD in the first place.

We can see by these examples that it is not one therapy that is the cure. It takes a group of specialists to heal a trauma survivor. In the case of my son, if I had stopped at the physician, we would not have detected the neck problem until it was very acute and would have caused even more damage by lack of treatment. If I had stopped at just the physician and the chiropractor, the negative charges shot into the body during the fight-or-flight response would not have been released and would have wound its way into the body, eventually causing mental, emotional, and physical problems. By taking him to all three therapists together and immediately, we got him healed quickly with no lasting negative aftereffects.

So what is the difference between the therapies? How do we know who to go to? First, it is really important to know what each therapy is capable of and what its scope and limits are. One of the worst ways to end up going to a therapist is purely on the recommendation of a friend who had good results for their unique problem, or through a therapist who automatically always refers to a particular therapist. Psychotherapists now often refer trauma clients to somebody who does EMDR (eye movement desensitization and reprocessing) therapy. Nobody I know with PTSD and who has tried it has ever had any really good lasting benefits from this therapy. Remember, it may not work for you! Each of our needs is different at various stages of recovery. Do your own research on the Internet if necessary. You and your body are the only ones that will ultimately know what the appropriate treatment for you is at any given time of the process. This is why I recommend a particular order of first-responder therapies. To heal efficiently from trauma, you must first have a healthy body (physician), then mental balance (psychologist/psychiatrist), and finally an emotionally cleared and reconnected body to make sound, logical healing choices for yourself in the future (I am recommending Trauma Touch Healing).

At present, the gap between the physician and the psychotherapist is disastrous and inexcusable. As a standard procedure, every physician treating a survivor of trauma should also be referring the patient to a psychotherapist or psychiatrist *before* the patient is discharged from his care. I hear time and time again of physicians releasing trauma survivors without even warning the patient about the emotional letdown they may experience when they are sent home again after hospital care.

For example, can you imagine being a burn survivor, with all the serious and complex issues related to that, and *never* being referred to a specialist psychologist to help with the mental issues that surface after discharge? In many cases this is presently true! It's really difficult to understand the ignorance and lack of understanding of the vital need for therapists to come together as a cohesive whole to treat trauma patients. Naturally, when survivors get home and reality sets in, they very quickly spiral into deep depression, often seriously contemplating suicide if not actually committing suicide. They need good psychotherapists trained to treat trauma or, in this case, psychotherapists who know how to treat burn survivors who have special, unique psychological needs! The omission of referring patients is a travesty and completely unnecessary!

We, as healers, should always be guiding those in our care onto the next best, appropriate therapist who can further assist in a survivor's continuing healing process. For this, physicians need to educate themselves on what the survivor's next needs are emotionally, as well as physically. We should always be asking ourselves, what is the next healing step for this patient physically,

The Emotional Release Process

mentally, and spiritually/emotionally? We cannot, as healers, continue to remain separate and stuck only in our own narrow healing modality. For a trauma survivor, there are many steps to go in the process of healing before resolution is reached. Be responsible healers, get educated, and refer!

Likewise, it is unethical and a travesty that psychotherapists and psychiatrists do not recommend their clients onto the next step of healing, which is the emotional clearing of the *body*, not just healing the mind. There are two aspects of emotional healing: mental and somatic. I see over and over that these particular therapists would rather keep a survivor trapped and continuing psychotherapy for years, often well after the therapist is aware that the therapy is no longer effective. Because the truth is that if the body tissue is not also cleared of the negative emotional electrical charges rooted from the trauma, over time, the survivor becomes emotionally stuck, gets depressed, and numbs the body from feeling. None of this is conducive to progressing forward in the healing process.

This is a place where I found myself. There are countless others who honestly have no idea what the next step should be. They are never properly advised, educated, or guided with information from the treating physician or therapist to ever know what's next in the healing process. This is so important, both mentally and emotionally, to know for trauma survivors especially. So why recommend Trauma Touch Healing as the first bodywork step in the healing process? Why not some other body therapy? Let's investigate some other therapies and quickly analyze them. The following are other types of bodyworkers (besides Somatic Experiencing, which we have already compared) who clients I know have been referred to for emotional release treatments.

Chiropractic: According to Spineuniverse, "chiropractors are medical professionals who diagnose and treat disorders of the musculoskeletal and nervous systems. Chiropractors believe one of the main causes of pain and disease is the misalignment of the vertebra in the spinal column (subluxation). Through the use of manual detection (palpation), carefully applied pressure, massage, and manual manipulation of the vertebrae and joints (adjustments), chiropractors are able to relieve pressure and irritation on the nerves, restore joint mobility, and help return the body's homeostasis."

Nowhere will you see that chiropractic care is appropriate for deep emotional release work. A chiropractor may learn emotional release work and add that education to chiropractic work, but purely as a chiropractor, this doctor's focus is not deep emotional release work from trauma.

Massage: According to About.com. Alternative Medicine, "massage therapists use long, smooth strokes, kneading and other movements focused on superficial layers of muscle using massage oil or lotion. Massage therapy improves circulation by bringing oxygen and other nutrients to body tissue. It relieves muscle tension and pain, increases flexibility and mobility, and helps clear lactic acid and other waste, which reduces pain the stiffness in muscles and joints."

Again, this is not the therapist to refer to for deep emotional release work, as there is virtually no training given for trauma treatment, emotional release work, or how to cope with it unless further specialized training is undertaken. Responsibly, massage therapists should refer to another therapist when it becomes obvious that a client would benefit from deep emotional release work instead of attempting to treat this client and further harming them. Massage, however, can be very beneficial after deep emotional release work to integrate the body's energy.

Yoga: According to the American Yoga Association, "Yoga: The word yoga means to *join or yoke together*, and it brings the body and mind together into one harmonious experience. The whole structure of yoga is built on three main structures: exercise, breathing, and meditation. Regular daily practice of all three parts of this structure of yoga produce a clear, bright mind and a strong, capable body."

Time and again I hear of survivors being encouraged to see the local yoga instructor for help with releasing trauma. Ugh! The yoga instructor, unless properly credentialed to do so, should not be treating trauma survivors in need of emotional release work—ever! I must emphasize that yoga instructors, in general, are not credentialed to work on the delicacy of emotional releasing rooted from trauma. Most have not studied bodywork, anatomy, physiology, pathology, or trauma from any accredited college in order to practice release work. Furthermore, unless they have graduated from an accredited college in some kind of bodywork and then specialized in trauma work, they are quite frankly treating way out of scope and are very dangerous to a survivor regarding re-traumatization. *After* emotional release work is completed, however, yoga would be highly beneficial for a trauma survivor.

Reiki: According to the International Center for Reiki Training, Reiki "is a Japanese technique for stress reduction and relaxation that also promotes healing. It is administered by 'laying on hands' and is based on the idea that an unseen 'life force energy' flows through us and is what causes us to be alive. If one's 'life force' energy is low, then we are more likely to get sick or feel stress, and if it is high, we are more capable of being happy and healthy."

Did you read anywhere that this is a modality for the treatment of negative emotional release work from body tissue rooted from trauma? No, you did not. Reiki has its place in energetic healing, but not specifically for the treatment of clients suffering the emotional after-effects of trauma plus all its issues and unique responses.

Acupuncture: According to the University of Maryland Medical Center, acupuncture "is a type of treatment based on Chinese medicine—a system of healing that dates back thousands of years. At the core of Chinese medicine is the notion that a type of life force, or energy, know as *qi* (pronounced chee) flows through energy pathways (meridians) in the body. An imbalance of *qi* (too much, too little, or blocked flow) causes disease. To restore balance to the *qi*, an acupuncturist inserts needles at points along the meridians. These acupuncture points are places where the energy pathway is close to the surface of the skin."

Again, this is not a modality focused on deep negative emotional release work for trauma. But once the heavy, negative emotions have been released from deep in the body tissue, acupuncture would be an excellent treatment to have to address residual physical pains and illnesses, harmony, energetic integration and the essential rebalancing of the *qi*.

Cranial Sacral Therapy: According to the Upledger Institute International, "cranial sacral therapy (CST) is a gentle, hands-on approach that releases tensions deep in the body to relieve pain and dysfunction and improve whole body health and performance. Using a soft touch, which is generally no greater that 5 grams, practitioners release restrictions in the soft tissue that surround the central nervous system. CST is increasingly used as a preventative health measure for its ability to bolster resistance to disease, and it's effective for a wide range of medical problems associated with pain and dysfunction."

I once took a course in cranial sacral therapy, so I can inform you firsthand that it can assist in unwinding trauma. However, its method of processing the unwind is completely different from Trauma Touch Healing and is not comprehensive enough to simultaneously help with all other issues of PTSD *and* keep the client safe during emotional releasing. In fact, during a practice session one day, a student had an enormous spontaneous emotional release complete with sobbing and hysterics while being worked on by another student. The poor student giving the therapy was completely spooked, because we were never warned this could happen (purgative response) or what to do if it did. The instructor, who was supposedly very experienced and had practiced cranial sacral therapy for years, did not appear to know what to do either. The unfortunate receiving student, who was probably badly re-traumatized, never came back to the class, and rightfully so. This therapy is simply not comprehensive enough to be specifically treating chronic trauma issues, and therapists are not trained how to correctly respond to emotional releases so as not to re-traumatize a trauma survivor. Cranial sacral therapy does not address dissociation, boundaries, rage, triggering or depression nor does it give any techniques to assist counteract these responses in a trauma client. Additionally, Trauma Touch Healing works with the Peripheral Nervous System as well as the Central Nervous System, and does not have to rely on the often suspect and unreliable intuitive *feeling* of very subtle body tides by the therapist. One benefit of cranial sacral work is working with trauma clients that cannot talk, such as babies and preverbal children. In this regard, Trauma Touch Healing cannot assist since it requires verbal communication between the client and the therapist. In these cases, I would refer a client to cranial sacral therapy.

So why then is emotional releasing so important? I suppose to really get the point across, we have to use an analogy. If you had a tree that was very sick and discovered that the problem was root fungus, after good assessment, the fungus problem must obviously first be healed before the tree could fully recover. Right? The outward symptoms of the root fungus problem may be multiple—lack of fruit on the tree, a scrawny-looking tree losing its branches and leaves, or a tree infested with predator insects taking advantage of its weakened state. All these symptoms can be the subsequent, physical outward results of root fungus. In this situation, if we did not initially correctly assess the root fungus problem and spent all our time fertilizing the tree to get more fruit and get it thriving again, would we succeed? No, because the cause of its non-thriving is the root fungus, and roots that are ill cannot absorb fertilizer properly. If we added more or less watering each day, would we succeed in making this tree healthy? No, because we need to treat the roots first before the water can be absorbed and properly regulate water needs. Will treating and spraying the tree for predator insects help it? No, because this is merely a natural result/symptom of the tree being sick and weak. Killing the insects in the tree is going to do nothing to help cure the tree roots, and while the tree

The Emotional Release Process

remains weak, it will always be vulnerable to predators and disease. So first we must always establish what the *root cause* of a physical symptom is; otherwise, there cannot ever really be a successful treatment.

If we established that root fungus was the root cause of all the trees symptoms, how would we treat this tree? Obviously, we must treat the root and successfully kill the fungus. Once the tree's roots are being treated successfully, now it would be appropriate to assist it to fully recover by pruning the branches, fertilizing the soil, getting its appropriate water needs corrected, and killing the predator insects until the tree was strong, healthy, and thriving again.

Similarly, what on earth is the success rate of curing a sick human if all we are doing is treating the symptoms? First we must go about establishing the *root cause* of the problem. If it is established that the *root cause* is negative emotional gunk caused by trauma sitting stuck and unreleased in the cells and tissues of the body causing disease, imbalance, and illness, the most logical action is to go to a therapist who knows how to release it. This is surely not difficult to grasp, is it? So why is it that we send trauma survivors with PTSD to therapists who do not really have a clue about emotional release work; how to teach techniques to control dissociation, anger, and depression; or how to help the survivor properly establish their boundaries again? Surely this must be done first before other bodyworkers can be effective?

Once the body has been successfully treated and cleared of the harmful negative charges, empowered again, and taught helpful, practical techniques to modify negative responses, there is then a plethora of therapists to refer a survivor to. These professionals can then have a positive effect on a survivor who has usually developed many physical and stress-related problems rooted from the initial trauma, as previously explained. Treating symptoms rooted from emotions experienced during trauma with an uneducated bodyworker is an exercise in futility and ineffectiveness. It wastes money for clients who must mostly pay out-of-pocket for alternative medicine treatments, and it often does nothing more than re-traumatize a client who is then worse off than before treatment.

We are entering a new, exciting paradigm in healing. As therapists, we must begin to streamline, change, and better the long process of healing trauma. While initially stabilizing a trauma survivor physically and mentally is good and necessary, our immediate next step must be to look for the *root cause* of developing physical and mental problems and treat that correctly first, as soon as possible. It is no longer valid for physicians to keep indefinitely treating the symptoms of their patients with prescription drugs and other physical therapies without also simultaneously trying to find out the root cause and referring the patient to the correct therapist to heal the identifiable root problem.

It is also no longer valid or responsible or ethical for psychotherapists and psychiatrists to keep treating a trauma survivor indefinitely, without also suggesting and referring their clients to the next or simultaneous step of healing. This step is clearing the body tissue and cells of recorded trauma memory at its quantum level—deep somatic emotional release therapy.

Similarly, it is highly unethical for bodyworkers and energy workers to take on trauma clients for treatment of emotional releasing unless they have undertaken the correct education to do so. Refer! If you do this, you have a much higher chance of retaining this client in the future than one you have just re-traumatized and who will, rightfully, never return to you for treatment again.

For trauma survivors, finding and identifying the *root cause* of their physical/mental problems is imperative for proper healing. Usually at the base or root of their physical and mental problems, especially those with chronic PTSD, are the negative emotions that have wound themselves deeply into their body cells and tissue over time through the neurological system, disrupting homeostasis and unbalancing the body. These emotions must be released, corrected, and reversed out before complete healing will or can ever take place. It has to be done! This, I believe, is the correct pathway in the emotional release process.

TEN

Ego: The Enemy of Healing

Probably the most fascinating feature of Trauma Touch Healing is how it is performed. It is an unassuming touch therapy where therapists are trained to step out of ego and have no prejudgments or expectations of the outcome. To do this, the therapist must know that he/she is not the one doing the therapy. There is no manipulating, no pushing of energy here and there, and no putting of energy in or pulling energy out of the body. In fact, there is no intending of any kind while touching the body. You are just there and present, allowing the client's body to make the decisions of how the emotional release process proceeds. The job of the therapist is to hold the space and keep the client safe from dissociation and fear by staying very focused and alert to any changes that may hurt a successful session outcome. Sometimes, this egoless way of treating is easier said than done! We are egotistical creatures, but in the healing world, real effort needs to be taken to put this aside for the sake of the one needing care. Otherwise, this ego can become detrimental to the client/patient, as we will see in some following real-life examples.

Probably the most damaging demonstration of ego, at present, is the lack of acceptance of each other's healing expertise. It is interesting. I spoke with a friend the other day who said he had met up with a local chiropractor. In passing conversation, my friend told the chiropractor he was being treated by a Trauma Touch Healer. The chiropractor laughed immediately and said to him, "Oh that stuff doesn't work." Excuse me? Without knowing anything about the modality or why the man was being treated, this so-called chiropractor unceremoniously dismissed one of the most vital and valuable therapies existing today in the treatment of those suffering from trauma and

PTSD. This is a perfect example of ego in its most insidious form! But I had to chuckle to myself. When looking up a definition of chiropractic care, it stated, "Traditional chiropractic assumes that a vertebral subluxation interferes with the body's innate intelligence, a vitalistic notion that brings ridicule from mainstream health care." Ah! A battle of the egos! In light of that, you would think this chiropractor would know better and have a different, open attitude to new ideas and therapies. Ego, unfortunately, encourages enormous ignorance.

On the other hand, when I was talking with a surgeon several months ago, he asked me what work I did. When I told him, he was very interested in hearing from me what it was all about, as he had never heard of Trauma Touch Healing. He listened carefully as I explained and he asked me if this had anything to do with energy work. I answered that indeed the emotions are tied up with the neurological system and our electrical light bodies; therefore, we could say that Trauma Touch Healing is a form of energy work. We parted ways, but at the end of the evening, he again approached me. He had obviously processed what I had told him and had spent some time thinking about it. He came up to me, grabbed my arm, and said, "Just keep doing what you are doing! I have been reading books and articles on energy work, and I think this is going to be huge in the future. Stay with it!" What wonderful encouragement from somebody in mainstream medicine! I was so surprised at his response that it got me thinking how wonderful it was that there really are some mainstream medical practitioners who are pushing forward, keeping an open mind, and willing to stretch their perimeters of medical understanding to encompass new ideas and theories in alternative medicine as the world moves into a new healing paradigm. They are willing to listen and at least mentally entertain new methods of healing. This, I think, is a beautiful example of a trained medical professional sidestepping ego and self-grandeur to rather let curiosity, open-mindedness, and learning rule the day! Out of the two examples above, who would you rather have treating you?

It must be clearly understood that when a healer of any kind gets wrapped up too tightly in their own ego, it narrows the mind. This is the cause of some very bad decisions-making. When the ego and arrogance of a practitioner causes him to think they know it all (God complex) and they fail to look with care at the health issues of a patient from an unselfish, humble, and unassuming point of view, serious mistakes can be made in diagnosis. Time and time again, I see this arrogance causing failure to follow the basic protocols

Ego: The Enemy of Healing

of medicine. An egotistic healer's false sense that they know without a doubt instead of following established procedure usually turns out very detrimental to the patient and is often deadly. The following are perfect examples of what happens when the healer decides to forego procedure, because he has decided, with complete assuredness, a diagnosis without the proper tests to support it.

A friend of mine had a young wife who was finally pregnant after months of fertility treatments. Very soon into the pregnancy he noticed a lump on her breast. Both, naturally concerned, asked the doctor to check out the lump and asked for his opinion. He apparently looked at it and immediately dismissed it as nothing to worry about. "Just a cyst," he said. As the lump grew in size, the couple asked another doctor and got a similar response. This time it was suggested that it was probably just a blocked milk duct. Nobody, it seemed, was willing to address the obvious concern that it may be breast cancer and test the lump appropriately!

By the time she gave birth, the lump was the size of a grapefruit. Only then did the doctor decide to do what he should have done immediately many months ago; he took a biopsy. It did turn out to be breast cancer, but too much time had elapsed and further testing revealed the cancer had already metastasized and spread to many other parts of her body. When her child was only eighteen months old, she finally succumbed to brain cancer. What were these doctors thinking? Shouldn't a good healer not assume but put all personal opinions aside and look at all the possibilities and eliminate the doubts by proper testing?

I had a similar experience, but through prior education and study, I knew better and fought. I had a pink, crusty spot on my wrist for about fifteen years. It never changed in size in all these years. Doctors had looked at it, and twice it had been frozen off. Nobody seemed concerned, and it always returned. A few years ago it suddenly had a dramatic growth spurt. I immediately grew very concerned, as it just seemed to be growing too aggressively, so I went back to the doctor who again decided it was nothing. He offered to freeze it off again if I wanted. I explained this had been done twice already only to grow back, but now it was behaving in an entirely different manner and growing very fast. All my inner alarm bells were ringing to get this taken care of. Only at my stubborn insistence did he refer me to a skin specialist.

I finally got the appointment I needed four months later, as the specialist was busy. When I finally arrived at my appointment, the spot had already tripled in size. I went through my history with the doctor, who then put on special magnifying glasses and closely inspected the spot. She then declared that it was nothing and said she could freeze it off. Then, she said, we could see what happens in the future with it and keep an eye on it. I had already informed her I had done this twice! I wanted a biopsy done. Why was she not listening to me? She made it clear a biopsy was unnecessary, and a battle of wills ensued. Only at my strong insistence did she eventually agree to do it but also added that the biopsy would leave a bad scar on my arm (to frighten me off?) and then I would see that the results would tell me it was nothing.

I got an urgent call two days later from the doctor telling me my spot had been diagnosed by the lab as a skin cancer called squamous cell carcinoma. I was to get into the office right away to discuss my treatment options. I never received an apology. All she ever said to me was, "It looked so innocuous!" What a response. Luckily, it had not yet reached the deeper layers of skin (it was in situ) and it was quickly taken care of in the next few months with a special cancer-fighting cream. I must add something relevant here, though. When I had done my own research on this cancer, I had discovered that the best biopsy would have been the punch biopsy, not the scrape biopsy she had done. She had also neglected to tell me that surgery was a possible option. On a subsequent appointment, I asked her why she had rather done a scrape biopsy and why she hadn't told me and discussed with me the surgical option. I remember her turning slowly and imperiously towards me, beady eyes fixed on mine, and she said, "My, we have been doing our homework, haven't we?" Yes, indeed doctor—my body, my life. *You* should have been doing your job to protect me far better and without the egotistical attitude! This also really reinforced to me that healers would be well served to listen more carefully to their patients regarding symptoms. We know our bodies best.

When I married my second husband, I found myself pregnant very quickly after our wedding. When I was about two-and-half months pregnant, however, I started spotting and called my gynecologist. He advised me to take a week off work and go on bed rest. I did this, but when the spotting still had not stopped, he suggested that I go to the hospital where he scheduled an ultrasound to find out what was going on. The result was that I was no longer pregnant. "Empty womb," the radiologist said. At some point, I had lost the baby. My doctor suggested to me that I'd had a miscarriage. I was baffled. When I argued that I am sure I would have felt or noticed this, he told me this is quite common. He explained that it often happens when going to the bathroom, and I probably hadn't noticed. I returned to work. Soon after, on

Ego: The Enemy of Healing

a Saturday morning, I developed an acute pain in my abdomen. Thinking I had eaten something not quite good, my husband, who was working all day, called a doctor friend of a friend who prescribed some pain pills for me. Despite the pain pills, the pain increased. By evening, I was in agony. A girlfriend, who was very concerned, came to sit with me and keep me company while I waited for my husband to arrive home later that night.

At about eight o'clock in the evening, I remember sitting on the couch and having a strange sensation which felt like two invisible hands pushing on my back, directing me to get up and walk toward the telephone. I felt like I was floating and starting to leave my body. It was a very strange feeling, like I was going away. I instinctively knew I was in serious trouble, and I was scared. I called the hospital and told them I thought something was very wrong, and I urgently needed the doctor. It was after-hours for the doctor, so the exchange informed me they had contacted him and I must meet him at the hospital right away, which was a half hour drive for me. I told my friend we needed to get to the hospital immediately, and I was grateful that she was there by my side so at least she would be able to drive. I was wrong! I had a stick-shift car, and she could only drive an automatic, which put me behind the wheel in very bad shape. I was really afraid I was going to pass out. I felt light-headed and was still in very acute pain. I drove, I prayed, I held together, and we somehow arrived at the hospital in one piece.

The emergency intake nurse took one look at me and asked me if I was always that pale. I didn't know how to answer her. I hadn't been looking at myself in the mirror, but I was apparently not looking very well. Fortunately, the doctor arrived not long afterward and did a syringe test into my uterus, which confirmed what he had probably already guessed—I was hemorrhaging internally. My husband arrived as they were getting me ready for emergency surgery. By then, I was already going into shock, feeling cold, and experiencing uncontrollable shivering. There was another problem. Because I was unprepared for surgery and had eaten some food about an hour prior, there was also concern for nausea and vomiting during and after surgery. With all this hanging over my head, I went into merciful oblivion and prayed to God to help me and protect me. I remember hearing an enormous roaring in my ears as the darkness came over me, and I succumbed to the anesthetic.

I awoke feeling very ill. My husband was there holding a cold, wet cloth to my forehead to help with the nausea. I was then told that I had experienced an ectopic pregnancy (a pregnancy that grows in the fallopian tube instead of the uterus). As the embryo had grown, it had burst the tiny tube. Because of the high density of blood supply to this area of a woman's body, the rupture had put my life in mortal danger. An undiagnosed ectopic pregnancy is a life-threatening situation and extremely dangerous for the patient. But wait! Had I not been diagnosed with an empty uterus and told I had had a miscarriage?

I had many questions, but I had to fight for my life first. The doctor informed me that my fitness level (from daily martial arts) had literally saved my life. The tightness of my muscles had slowed the bleeding enough that I had not passed out first, which often happens in such cases. When women pass out from the hemorrhaging, it usually takes too long to figure out what's wrong with them. Because they cannot tell you their symptoms, this often leads to death before diagnosis. So I had been lucky once again! However, my body had taken a serious beating and was reacting. I had a high temperature and fever, and my kidneys had shut down. While I was not in ICU, I was undergoing high care, and nurses were coming by every half hour to take my vitals and get me to drink as much water as possible to encourage my kidneys to start functioning again. At day two, I was still not passing any urine.

There was another huge problem for me. It was 1982, and the doctor, who was obviously very concerned, told me there was a disease that had no name yet. However, they had determined it was being passed to people through intravenous blood. I was in need of a blood transfusion, but he was discouraging me from taking it because of the danger of possible contamination, as they did not have more information or tests at that time to correctly screen the blood for this unknown disease. The disease in later years earned a name—AIDS. Fortunately, I never took the blood, because the doctor felt I was young and strong enough to replace my own blood over time. I really think this was the only thing he ever did correctly in my entire doctor/patient relationship with him. Again, I was very lucky!

By day three, my body was starting to respond to treatment. After five nights in the hospital, I was finally discharged. Still in pain from the major abdominal surgery, I began the six-week recovery period at home. I was not able to work or drive. During this time, I had a follow-up consultation with the doctor. I asked him what should be done about birth control once I had recovered. He explained that I had lost one fallopian tube, and because ovulation takes place once a month from alternating tubes, I only had a 50 percent chance of getting pregnant. His advice was to take no precautions, because it would take longer to get pregnant again. He was wrong again! Only eight

Ego: The Enemy of Healing

weeks after discharge, I was pregnant again. The pregnancy was a healthy one, but it was decided to perform a cesarean birth, because the ectopic pregnancy surgery had been so recent. I was also very concerned about the physical stresses of giving birth naturally with the recent abdominal incision. So another major surgery was scheduled.

It was during the surgery to deliver my son that another example of the negative effects of ego happened. After my son was safely in the hands of the nurses in charge, the doctor attempted to suction and clean out the surgical area before closing up and discovered that the assistant surgical nurse had forgotten to plug in the suction machine. Irritated, the doctor asked my husband, who was watching the surgery, to assist in the suction process. So while the nurse plugged in the machine, my husband, a lay person who was not properly scrubbed up for surgery, suctioned out my abdomen to the delight and amusement of the doctor and the embarrassment of the nurse. I mention this because after another five-day stay in the hospital, I was discharged but was not feeling well. When I stood up, I was so dizzy I almost fell over. The discharge nurse, very concerned, told me she had reported this to doctor and wanted to wait and hear what he decided first before discharging me. Shortly after, without another word, I was discharged.

I was just never well after this birth. I felt weak and tired. I spent many months just lying in bed and attending to the baby. I developed severe asthma, which I was treated for. I was struggling to breastfeed and finally had to stop at three months when my milk supply simply gave out. I was very disappointed with this. After five months, I finally started to recover and regain my strength. About a year later, during a routine examination with an internist, he asked me if I had been aware that I'd had a recent blood infection. He had found the infectious footprints in the blood sample he'd taken. I told him I was not aware of it at all, but a lot of my postnatal illness started to make sense. Should the gynecologist have done a simple blood test before my discharge from the hospital to make sure I was healthy? I believe a good, humble, highly professional and focused doctor would have done this. Is this not what we deserve when we have to put ourselves in the hands of a healer?

Relating to the ectopic pregnancy, a year after the birth of my son, I went back to the radiation department at the hospital where the ultrasound was done and asked the radiologist how they had missed the ectopic pregnancy. His answer stunned me! He explained there is a standard procedure/protocol in place that when a patient is diagnosed with an empty uterus after a confirmed pregnancy, the patient's doctor should immediately order a blood test to recheck for pregnancy. If the blood test still confirms a pregnancy, this would indicate that the embryo is growing in a fallopian tube. In my case, why was this not done? For the sake of a simple blood test, this doctor had put my life in serious danger. What was he thinking? I believe this was another perfect example of ego at its worst. He had just decided I'd had a miscarriage and was so sure of his diagnosis, apparently, even though I could not confirm a miscarriage, that he had chosen his decision over the simple standard medical protocol in place to protect my life. It just hadn't occurred to him that he may be wrong. This lack of professionalism, good sound medical reasoning, and normal procedure to ensure my safety had resulted in a very dangerous, life-threatening situation for me and had caused havoc with my life and health!

By then, I was quickly learning that the ego and arrogance of a practitioner can easily turn detrimental and sometimes deadly for a trusting patient. When I found myself pregnant again with my second son, I did not intend to have this doctor treat me. I found a wonderful gynecologist who was professional, humble, and very caring. I went on to have a crisis-free delivery, a healthy postnatal recovery, and many months of breastfeeding my child!

Ego—the enemy of healing. It's something to be very carefully considered. If you are also experiencing this, move on to somebody else as soon as possible. There are wonderful, professional healers out there who are devoid of egotism. We should seek them out. I would like to share two more examples—one about an egotistical yoga instructor and another about a massage therapist choosing to treat out of scope.

I was waiting for a client one day when I bumped into a local yoga instructor who had heard of my work with trauma and said she was interested in asking me some questions about it. She went on to tell me she had six or seven yoga clients who were trauma survivors, and she was working with them and encouraging them to release their negative emotions. I was very surprised, because most yoga instructors are obviously not trained for this work. Feeling great concern for her clients, I asked her what her educational background was with trauma. She said, "Well, after talking with you, I think I may like to go and study this." She asked me if I thought they would accept her.

"Well," I said, "First you would need to be a physical bodywork therapist of some kind, certified and graduated from an accredited school. You would

Ego: The Enemy of Healing

also need to show you were proficient at the bodywork with several years' experience. Then you could apply to study Trauma Touch Healing. To become certified would take longer time and resources and would involve conducting clinic work from your own established office with a minimum of three clients. You would be required to work with a psychologist and a mentor while sending weekly written reports and being closely monitored by Chris Smith in Colorado to successfully gain certification."

When she heard this, she said, "Oh, I don't have any of that, so I guess I can't go and study it." From this conversation, it didn't seem to occur to her at all that it may actually take great care and special training to work with trauma survivors, especially those with PTSD. Her lack of knowledge, appreciation, or care regarding the seriousness of what she was doing in attempting to treat these clients without *any* of the proper credentials, was astounding—and scary! This is truly ego at its best! It was more important for her to feel good about saying she had all these needy trauma clients that she was supposedly helping. What help? Tragically for trauma survivors, this attitude is not an isolated one.

My next example happened with a client I had been working on for close to three months. She was nearing the end of the course for trauma therapy, and I had worked very hard to keep her grounded and balanced during the delicate and difficult process. As is usual at this point of the therapy, she felt the need to do some integration work on her body and asked me if it would be alright to have somebody give her a massage. I told her that would be good as long as it was only a relaxing swedish massage and not blended with any kind of energy work. That, I explained, would be very detrimental to our work at this point.

She returned to therapy the following week looking disorientated. Dismayed at how she looked, I asked her what had happened during the week. She told me she had gone to the massage therapist for a swedish massage, but at the end of the massage, he had done some energy work on her. I was in disbelief and asked her what he did. She didn't know. I asked her if he had asked her permission. "No," she said. I asked why she hadn't stopped him. She told me she had her eyes closed and never realized he was working on her energetically until she opened her eyes and asked what he was doing.

This therapist was clearly somebody who felt no responsibility to stay in scope with what his client has requested and who felt perfectly comfortable doing whatever to a trusting client without permission, history, or proper intake as long as he felt it was necessary. It probably made him feel good and important doing energy work. With good training, in the bodywork world, this behavior is not condoned. It is highly unethical and very dangerous to clients, especially without an intake to find out what other treatments this client might also be undergoing at the moment and for what. This is also highly unprofessional and egotistical. When looking for a healer, I suggest using great discernment on whom you allow to treat you. Do your research!

Are we getting the picture? There are countless stories like those we just read. With all of this ego, ineptness, lack of acceptance and respect of each other's healing expertise, patients are the ones falling through the cracks every day. As a result, they are often badly hurt, re-victimized, and re-traumatized. I hope that with these few examples we have proved that ego, arrogance, and assuming are not compatible with good healing!

ELEVEN

Trauma Healing within Mainstream/Alternative Medicine: What Is Wrong?

Are you just as frustrated as I am to see the doctor reaching once again for the prescription pad to try yet another drug to solve a medical problem? Am I the only one who is disappointed at the five-to-ten-minute consultations? Yes, we have all heard the reason for this is the heavy medical malpractice insurances a doctor is forced to carry because of all the lawsuits out there. They are forced to cram as many patients in their day as possible to pay for it. But are they trying to change this so the patient can be given better care? Why do we continue to allow drug companies and medical insurance companies to keep us in bondage, pushing drugs on us and deciding which practitioners we can or cannot see? Why can't mainstream and alternative medicine combine their knowledge successfully? Wouldn't this be a vast improvement for patients if each understood, or at least respected, each other's healing skills? What is the problem? Here is what I think is intrinsically wrong.

The following is an interesting recorded question and answer session between a skeptical scientist and a spiritual master. I thought the conversation was very relevant to understanding the basic differences between mainstream medicine and the fundamentals of alternative medicine. The following excerpt is taken from a book called *Spiritual Perspectives, Volume 1* by the Radha Soami Satsang Beas Society.

Q. Was there a creator of the creation?

A. The Lord created this whole creation and shared the same life which he had with his creation. His creation is living because he has shared that life force with it. Nothing existed before the creation and nothing exists which he has not created. So he has created everything.

Q. Does this not seem to contradict the evidence which has resulted from scientific research into the human mind?

A. It is the research of Christ; it is the experience, the spiritual experience of all the mystics. Of course, we are human, and the research has been made at our level; but Christ says that having come to this level, we have access to the Father. This is the spiritual experience that mystics try to share with us in their scriptures or books. Just as scientists or philosophers share their experience and experiments in their books, so similarly the saints or the mystics also have experienced certain things within themselves which they share with us in their scriptures.

Q. It may be that they have seen something, but they show very little proof of it.

A. Well, you must test and prove it for yourself. You see, scientists tell you that a certain combination will give a certain result. You will say, "I have no proof of it." But you can have proof by doing it yourself—testing it for yourself. In the same way, you can also do research on the basis of the given formula. Then, only then, will you be convinced of the accuracy of the formula. Similarly, the spiritual experiences which the saints share with us in books and scriptures can only convince us when we try to follow their teachings, live their teachings, and make our own research according to these teachings. Then we can say whether they are right or wrong. How can we tell, otherwise unless we give them a fair trial?

Q. I'm not convinced.

A. Because you have not made any research within yourself.

Q. Maybe.

A. You see, in our very presence, scientists have gone to the moon, and we who have heard about it believe that they have gone to the moon. But if you had never heard about it, you might say, "I am not convinced that they have gone to the moon." Well, you may think whatever you like, but ...

Q. No such experimental proof exists about the soul.

A. What is in the body now that gives it life? The body is the same after death, so what is missing that it cannot move around? I'll tell you what gives life to this flesh.

Q. Maybe that's the creation of a new life, soul.

A. That is what I'm asking. What leaves the body and what comes into the body which gives it life?

Q. There may be nothing.

A. If there is nothing, then how is it that today we are running about and tomorrow we are dead? What is in the body? After all, there must be something in the body which gives us life and something in the body without which the body becomes useless. What is that? I mean, as a scientist, you must have made such research. What is it? Give it any name. You can't just say coincidentally you are living and coincidentally you are dead. There's something which is giving you life, something which, when taken out of the body, leaves the body useless. After you are dead, the body is still made up of the same elements as when you were alive: earth, water, fire, air and ether. The elements remain the same. So what is there that is missing from the body when we are dead?

Q. Maybe you are right.

This is a perfect example of the huge chasm in the understanding of human life. Our basic understanding or belief of life dramatically alters how we view medical science. If we think that the human body is only that which can be seen with the naked eye or only that which can be detected under a microscope, then we severely limit ourselves on understanding the full scope of human life and how it heals. Mainstream medicine does not believe in the existence of an energy force that gives life to the human body simply because it cannot actually be seen.

Alternative medicine believes that this life force is the very foundation of life and breathes life into all aspects of the physical body. Without it, the human body would not have life at all. It also acknowledges that this energy has an innate intelligence that trumps our limited minds. Alternative medicine recognizes that each person's energy also has an individual blueprint that can become blocked and damaged by traumatic life experiences. This also needs to be corrected and healed. Because a blueprint is always the foundation, it makes good sense that this also must be treated at some point, or full healing cannot take place. Therefore, it must be acknowledged.

The emotional body (abstract and unseen) is connected to the neurological system of the physical body (seen). Both operate by electrical currents. But while the neurological system gets its electricity from the energetic blueprint (soul, spirit), the soul energy is plugged into and gets its electricity from the outer universe, which is alive with connecting, vibrating atoms breathing life into everything. To some, this seems far-fetched, unbelievable, and a source of ridicule. To others, this esoteric unseen world is as tangible as any object and makes complete sense.

Regardless of what you believe, some of us have been trained for eons in higher spirit regions to work in the healing arts of individual energy fields—how to heal them, balance them, unblock them, and repair them again. In alternative medicine, you will see many practitioners offering all kinds of different energetic healing. It is wise then to do your homework before placing yourself in the hands of any kind of energy practitioner. Like any healer, find out if this is a genuine one, what their work achieves, and whether it's suitable for your needs. In all areas of healing, there are good and bad practitioners. Many feel important saying they can do energy work but really don't know how to do it properly to keep a client safe. If you ever feel you are in the hands of an incompetent practitioner and not feeling good after sessions, don't hesitate to leave immediately and seek out somebody better.

Because trauma has such a profound negative effect on the entire neurological system and our attached emotions, it must be healed correctly and proficiently to regain ourselves again. Without this particular treatment, a victim will never heal in a complete way. So who will work on the somatic emotions after the physical body has healed and the mind has been balanced? Again, physicians don't do this work and mostly scoff that it exists anyhow. Psychotherapists and psychiatrists don't do this work either and also scoff at energetic healing in general because they don't understand it. Alternative medicine is the only place you can turn to for healing the somatic emotional symptoms that results from the enormous impact of holding negatively charged emotions in the body after trauma. These must be let go, as we have said before.

I think that for many people the concept of the *spirit/soul* being housed in the body and supplying it energy can be a difficult one to grasp and comprehend. But when you believe in the soul and universal energy, it becomes easier. Then we must also question the source of this energy. It must come

Trauma Healing within Mainstream/Alternative Medicine: What Is Wrong?

from somewhere. Some believe that we (individuals) are all sparks of the divine supreme Creator energy who sent us out individually into the universe, so it could experience life through us. In the dimension where we exist, each energetic drop of this divine energy is housed in a physical body and gives it life. If this is true, then each of us possesses within us a spark of universal energy that sustains us. If each spark or drop comes from the Creator and is a perfect duplicate of this Creator energy source, then all of us also possess within us an intelligence equal to that of the supreme energy source that created us and all of life! This is awesome to think about. So what if there was a way to tap into this energy source in the body and ask it questions about healing? Do we think that we, with our limited minds, would know better than the universal Creator intelligence what a body needs to heal with our very limited, third-dimensional Intelligence? If we think with our physical brains that we are more intelligent than the universal Creator energy, then we are just being blindly egotistical. This is food for thought.

And why is believing in an intelligent universal energy that gives our physical bodies life a source for ridicule by mainstream medicine anyhow? If we analyze it, how do electrons spin around the nucleus of an atom? What energy spins them around? Aren't our bodies made up of millions of cells and atoms? If we split an atom, we know it releases a powerful energetic light. We have already learned how to use this powerful light energy to destroy (nuclear explosions), but did it occur to scientists that this same energy can also be used to heal? That there are beings in the universe (and yes, some are walking on our planet today) who know how to use this energy to heal the emotional/energy body that is affected and damaged during the experience of trauma? That there are healers who possess this knowledge? So what is the ridicule about?

There was a long period of time when we believed that the earth was flat until finally it was proven to be round. Because we believed the earth was flat, did it make it so? No. All the time we believed it was flat, the reality was that it was always round. Just because something is beyond our understanding and cannot be clearly seen, does not mean it doesn't exist! To take a narrow, stubborn stance that we must continue healing in old, outdated ways and forms and always ridicule new healing techniques, possibilities, and ideas that emerge is really *un*intelligent. Can we not step into new, better healing paradigms? Move forward? We owe it to those who need these healing techniques, old and new, to examine them and learn about them with an open mind, even if they are beyond our present understanding. Ridiculing new ideas that emerge without investigation is not beneficial to anybody.

We must accept that all healers have their limits and scopes, but together and integrated, we are the most effective in healing our patients/clients. This especially applies to trauma survivors who experience enormous complications on every level in the aftermath. For complete healing to ever take place, we must be able to use every resource available to us, physically, mentally, emotionally, and spiritually. It is our right as exquisite universal beings housed in human bodies to have available to us every aspect of healing to solve medical problems. To help our clients and patients have access to all aspects of healing, we, as healers, must also understand the various aspects. We must begin to break down the barriers and issues of separation and trust that exist today between mainstream and alternative medicine. These barriers only serve to keep those in need bound in ignorance and illness for the sake of our own laziness, stupidity, lack of interest, ego, and selfish desires. Is this really the way we want to continue to treat our ill clients who so desperately need our help?

To come together for a rounded, holistic healing of our clients, mainstream medicine must begin to open up to new exciting possibilities regarding the human body and how it fully functions, both physically *and* energetically. Alternative medicine must also know and realize that we cannot work only with the energetic body. We must know and respect when it is appropriate to refer those in our care to other healers, often in mainstream medicine, who are experts for physical and mental problems that have developed from the energy body being damaged. This too takes education and is essential.

The physical human body is a combination of body, mind, and spirit. When it gets injured in *any* way, all three aspects are affected, and each aspect needs focused time and specialists to help it to heal. The sooner we become aware of this, acknowledge this, educate ourselves, and start working together as a cohesive whole as healers, the sooner the methods and the way we heal will also begin to improve immensely! Our clients/patients can only benefit from this. What have we got to lose?

And so this book was written for those frustrated trauma survivors who have had their pathways to complete healing blocked one way or another. If you have not been receiving the knowledge you need to progress in your healing, it is my hope that now you can become more proactive in your own treatments, armed with powerful information. Now you have choices. Do your homework, dig on the computer for information about suggested treatments, and find out what they do. Find the courage when not being helped anymore by a practitioner to say "stop!" and move on to others who can do a better job to help in your progress. For the trauma survivors, it is not enough to just survive. Shout out, "I want and need and deserve to *thrive*!" You really can do this; it is your right! Now you've had placed in your hands some powerful tools and weapons—secrets revealed to successfully crack the PTSD code and tame your mystical dragon.

Epilogue

It is finished! I have written over many months and during trips to South Africa, Jordan in the Middle East, and America. I now sit in beautiful Southern California in the little Carlsbad Library on Carlsbad Village Drive, typing the end. It is two days before the New Year 2012, and I have said that this book will be completed before January 1. It will be!

I am thrilled but also emotional, because so much of this book is my heart and passion on the subject of trauma recovery. Plus, I am filled with so much empathy and compassion for those survivors still caught in the insidious and frustrating cyclic vortex of PTSD. It is my greatest wish that this book reaches the hands of every trauma survivor who has sent desperate pleas of help to the universe for assistance with their healing. I think this book would say, "You are not going unheard! There is hope, there is a way!"

This book, I hope, provokes new thought and introduces a vital therapy that is not yet widely known. In my opinion, the current general ignorance and lack of understanding regarding how important and vital proper integrated treatment is for trauma survivors has suspended or halted the healing of millions of trauma survivors. This is especially true in the sequence of *when* to treat the somatic emotional aspect of trauma trapped in the body cells and tissue. Countless others have taken their own lives in utter defeat and hopelessness. To have complete treatment, we must address a holistic approach and the combined healing aspects of body, mind, and emotion/spirit. Each relies upon the other, and no aspect can be left out or can be considered more important. Each aspect has its own specialists who are trained to treat survivors. Survivors, seek them out with this newfound knowledge. Healers, know your ethical scope and boundaries of treatment, and when you have reached your limits, refer to another healer for the betterment of your client!

There is nothing more powerful than knowledge that gives you the power of choice. Nobody can ever force somebody to undergo treatments he doesn't want. On the other hand, there are so many confused people who need further treatment and want to really get better in a complete way, but don't know their way through the maze of practitioners. It is my hope that this book also simplifies and makes the choices of treatment for trauma much clearer for the average person. I wish so much that somebody had placed this book in my hands thirty years ago! How much quicker I would have recovered.

While in South Africa, I found and read a book called *Inside Belsen* by Hanna Levy-Hass. It's about her personal experiences as a Jewish woman in the concentration camp in Belsen during World War II. On page 120 of the book, she is being interviewed about her experiences. I quote one of her remarks about the health of holocaust survivors, which is one of the most concise, accurate, and eloquent answers I have ever read.

> *In a very forthright speech, with the political content of which everybody certainly did not agree, Gideon Hausner, chief prosecutor in the Eichmann trial, said: "It is not just a matter of the slaughter of the six million who are no longer with us. Even more tragic is that those who are left are sick. It is a sickness that has infected the whole of mankind, a trauma that has inflicted deep wounds on the soul of man."*

> *With the liberation in 1945 many who had lived through all this were saved, but neither they nor their families are normal people any more. Neither their physical nor their mental health is intact, and if you ask me what effect it has had on their lives, I can only say that it has left scars which grow deeper and deeper as time goes on. Those I know suffer more and more and their ailments get worse and worse. We cannot say that the majority regained their strength and their power to work. They all made an effort to recover and lead a more or less normal life, but no one succeeded, I can assure you.*

If this book has served its purpose well, then the above description should now be more understandable. PTSD is a condition that needs the excellent skills of multiple healers if it has any hope of reversal. Without proper intervention, it is a condition that just gets worse with time. There are definitely various grades of trauma. There are some traumas that are more severe than others and have a great deal more of a devastating effect on a survivor, requiring many more years of therapy than another. This is true. But what I see has been missing, regardless of the grade of severity, is a more comprehensive and holistic approach to healing trauma. PTSD is one condition where we, as healers, cannot afford to just sit in our own individual modalities with blinders on if we are to be of any real help to a trauma survivor experiencing serious problems. We must become more educated about other modalities and be more aware of the conditions and symptoms of PTSD, so we can safely treat or knowledgeably refer survivors to the therapist who will be the most effective for them at any given stage of their recovery.

Some of the following trauma survivor groups would benefit enormously from learning about deep negative emotional release bodywork such as Trauma Touch Healing.

Addictions

Many years ago, I was shocked when a friend going through Alcoholics Anonymous told me that the success rate of kicking the habit was at best 5 percent! I was horrified. Those are not good odds. I wondered at the time what happened to the other 95 percent? How depressing to be sent or make the decision to put yourself in rehab knowing your chances of recovery are so dismal. I haven't heard of any better odds of recovery from other drug rehab facilities. So far, the only treatments I have heard of are the same as everything else: techniques to treat symptoms, psychotherapy, and relaxation. People who develop addictions usually have severe emotional problems that often stem from really bad life experiences. Once again, only treating the symptoms of addiction and giving them psychotherapy in most cases is not enough to do the trick. Asking somebody who is caught in the cyclic vortex of PTSD to relax with yoga and meditation is unrealistic. At best, these are short-term solutions. Addictions to drugs, alcohol, food, etc. are an attempt by the addict to dissociate. Any addiction is an unhealthy way they have discovered to temporarily feel better. When the good feeling wears off, it must be repeated. Unfortunately, after awhile, the repetitive drug use (habit) and the effects that the various drugs of choice has on the body also become addictive. You need more and more! The negative cycle has begun.

The problem is that if we are always looking at the top of the iceberg for our answers to solve the puzzle, we miss the bigger of picture of where it began and how it formed. All of the above therapies are good and necessary for immediate assistance. However, they are not comprehensive or deep enough to really help addicts permanently change. We cannot continue to ignore treatment of the root causes. Why not add deep somatic negative emotional release work for addicts and monitor the success rates after that? Maybe we would see an improvement in the odds. Is it not worth looking into and trying? What do we have to lose? Nothing. And we have everything to gain!

Cancer Society

While much progress has been made with cancer patients, negative emotional release work is an aspect I never hear patients referred to when I have talked to relatives of those who have succumbed to cancer. One of my friends told me that on the alternative medicine side of treating cancer, patients are referred to yoga, Reiki, acupuncture, and chiropractic and told to think positive, happy thoughts. What they are not guided toward is somebody who can assist in clearing out the old, negative emotional gunk in the body cells. This gunk causes severe imbalance, which impairs the immune system, ultimately resulting in the body's symptomatic expression of dis-ease—in this case, cancer.

For example, if you read *You Can Heal Your Life* by Louise Hay, she explains the emotional mental *probable cause* of cancer. According to *her* research cancer is rooted from: "Deep hurt. Longstanding resentment. Deep secret or grief eating away at the self. Carrying hatreds. "What's the use?" If these feelings can be identified as a cancer victim's probable emotional cause, what therapy are you directing them toward to help with *this* aspect? It seems to me that clearing out this hate, anger and despondency from the body tissues would have an enormously positive, helpful impact for those wanting to survive the disease!

What is the point of trying to eradicate and treat cancer with physical therapies, diet, and relaxing exercises when the *root cause* is never even addressed? Think happy thoughts when you are in the fight of your life? Not sure how happy I could feel while my body was being overstressed and ravaged by abnormal cells. Really! However, once emotional negative emotions are cleared out of the body, you naturally, automatically, and genuinely feel happy and light, because the emotions are dramatically shifted and transformed from negative to positive. Homeostasis will now no longer be overwhelmed, and the body will regain its balance. The neurological system would begin to heal, and the immune system could now recover and strengthen. After clearing the cause of the effect (cancer), all further and ongoing therapies have a much better chance of really working, taking hold, and being successful. Then diet, massage, meditation, and yoga techniques are excellent add-ons to further aid the body in recovery. Is this not at least worth a try in the treatment of cancer?

Burn Survivors

One of the most frustrating moments I have ever had was listening to how burn survivors are treated. Most survivors are not even given a referral to the psychotherapist when they finally leave the hospital after months of physical treatments and surgeries. This is unbelievable! While the hospital staff cheerily waves good-bye and tells the burn victim them how good he looks, absolutely nobody prepares the survivor for the huge emotional letdown of going home and being thrust out into the world again. Of all the people who have suffered trauma, these survivors especially need to have a referral to a specialist psychologist in-hand when they leave the hospital, so they have somebody to call when extreme depression sets in.

Further talking to burn survivors, they have received very little education on the different aspects of healing and their importance. Nothing is known or discussed about the progression of PTSD, how to recognize its symptoms, and the ways to seek help for this. While, of course, all care is initially concentrated on the physical burn problems, afterward there is little attention focused on the mental and emotional release aspects of healing other than support talk groups, which definitely have their limits as a therapy. Presently, burn healing is controlled by physicians and nurses who are too occupied with the physical aspect to realize how desperately the emotional aspects (mental and somatic) must also be addressed.

Without mental stability, these survivors don't do well and often still face years of continued surgeries and recoveries! Without mental balance and stability first, a therapist cannot even go in and perform the negative emotional release work. I have noticed that these survivors are very stuck in the cyclic vortex of PTSD and mentally/emotionally preoccupied with their victimization. As a result, they become very emotionally armored. This is a group who really needs good education explaining why it is so vitally necessary to also treat their emotions, both mentally and somatically. This emotional education should start in the hospitals. It is not.

After attending a group meeting of burn survivors, I did pick up an interesting group attitude. They do believe that a therapist treating them must also have had experience being a burn survivor. This is interesting and very much limits their recovery. First, releasing negative emotions out of the body of a client does not require a therapist to have experienced every kind of trauma that is being treated. You are simply releasing what is already there, regardless of the type of trauma. For example, the therapist does not have to know what it feels like to be a burn victim to assist you in releasing this memory from the body tissue. However, I think it is beneficial to have experienced trauma and PTSD to know the process all trauma survivors go through, regardless of the trauma.

I blame this lack of education on those who initially surround burn victims to save them. Once released from the hospital, these survivors need so much more than group talks to really help! At least one person in the small group where I was invited to speak has already taken his life, and another has seriously considered it. Not surprising! A strong suggestion to the organizers of the burn survivor talk groups: while group talks are very good, they have their limits and do not help survivors gain back their lives from PTSD. It's best to get better educated on *all* burn survivor needs, physically, mentally, emotionally, and spiritually. Then get some donated funds, if you can, for all these further treatments, especially for negative emotional release work, which medical insurances don't yet cover. Point the way and encourage burn survivors to try it! Please!

Military

If I was shocked to learn of the limited help for burn survivors, my discoveries and subsequent thoughts on how the military is presently been treated for war trauma is best described in one word: *appalling*! First, it is not helpful to your military career to report you are having symptoms of PTSD. Lately, we send our military men and women for multiple tours into one of the most stressful and traumatic environments like they are made of steel instead of highly attuned, sensitive beings. Then, unrealistically, we expect them to remain emotionally unscathed in the aftermath! And if they have been affected, they cannot talk about it to anyone in the military, because once they become labeled as having PTSD, it must be reported to their superiors. As a result, they are in a very real danger of losing their jobs. What kind of system is this? Don't we owe them much, much more?

I met a young marine who spent some time talking to me about his per-

Epilogue

sonal situation. Unfortunately, it is a common story. He is presently on his fifth tour in the Middle East. Before he left, he told me that he is unable to sleep for more than ninety minutes at a time. He is an alcoholic and has been taking all sorts of self-prescribed drugs to help him relax and sleep, but even these no longer work. Chronically exhausted, obviously hyperstressed, and experiencing daily flashbacks, the only way he knows to numb his mind is by reaching for the alcohol bottle and passing out. Of course, he is still expected to perform his military duties as a commander and is haunted daily, wondering whether decisions he makes during battle are good ones or are going to get soldiers under his command hurt or killed. When he is highly triggered in stressful situations, he cannot think clearly. He realizes this and feels guilty about it. It's a horrible, nightmarish existence for sure!

His marriage has already disintegrated; he lives alone and from prior experience knows he cannot even have a roommate for fear of what he may do to someone during his many flashbacks, blackouts, and drunken rages. Naturally, I asked him what help he was receiving from the military. He produced from his wallet something that looked like a business card cut from a piece of paper. This was the help! Laughing bitterly, he told me I could keep it. I went on this website listed on the card, and basically, it's an anonymous phone chat line with so-called trained professional counselors who talk about stress-related issues with you. Here is the perfect example of giving a desperate trauma survivor a hosepipe to put out the bushfire! I will share this website with you. It is dstressline.com. Go on there and judge for yourself if this would suffice after putting yourself in the shoes (if you can) of somebody with serious post traumatic stress disorder problems and needing real help. Shame on us! Is this really the best we can do? In the case of our returning veterans, it seems to me that a good, solid, realistic grasp of understanding and treating PTSD at our Veterans Administration level, is either completely misunderstood (very hard to believe) or just being intentionally and conveniently ignored, which is a very disturbing thought.

In the location where I live, I am surrounded by the Navy, Air Force, and Marines, and yet I got nowhere calling the VA military hospital in San Diego and asking if I could let returning soldiers know about Trauma Touch Healing. I was told to send a letter explaining what it is with some business cards, and they would put it in a folder for veterans who were seeking help to look at. Could I come and give a free lecture, I asked? No, I was told. Could I come to see somebody there and explain what the work entails and the benefit to veterans? No, I was not allowed to come to the hospital. As requested, I did send a package to the hospital. I have never gotten a reply that it was received and don't know if it ever made it into the folder for veterans to look at. I have also never heard from any veterans.

Somebody also told me about a local group that receives donations to help returning veterans with PTSD issues pay for therapy. I had heard this group was sending veterans to massage therapy and the chiropractor. Knowing these would not be much permanent help to somebody suffering from acute PTSD, I called to offer my services as a Trauma Touch Healer. At least in this case, I did get a call back, not from the director but from a subordinate who asked me several questions about the modality. A big question seemed to be about who I was affiliated with. I had no idea what that meant. I never heard from them again.

I did, however, hear from a wife sometime later that her veteran husband had been sent to a chiropractor through this group. He felt he was getting worse and had subsequently ended up in hospital for a week after becoming very triggered after a few sessions. This did not surprise me. Both were very upset and earnestly looking for real assistance. They wanted to try Trauma Touch Healing but could not afford the treatments. This group, with their donated funds, would not sponsor it or even sit down to listen to a presentation I would have gladly given. So, yet another veteran amongst thousands has fallen through the cracks and is being offered a hosepipe to put out the bushfire!

Lastly, I must share this. In 2008, I received a call from the spouse of a veteran who informed me that shock treatments were being used on returning veterans to control PTSD. What?! I could not believe it! I made some calls and verified that this was indeed true. I can only imagine the chain of command that this decision traveled through to become a VA treatment and how many doctors gave their nod of approval to the treatment.

I am not a doctor, but I do know that when a human mind is stuck wide open in fight-or-flight and in hyperarousal, the last thing it probably needs is to be electrically shocked! It is not surprising that these poor veterans also end up very ill and in the hospital after treatments like this. Are we stuck in the Dark Ages? What is the VA thinking? In this modern age, is this really the best we can come up with to treat our returning veterans who have been bravely protecting our freedoms? We should feel utter shame! Doesn't the VA think that perhaps it's time to revamp its protocol on treating trauma and post traumatic stress disorder and make every effort to find treatments that are truly beneficial? Or is it a question of resources they are not willing to spend on a burnt-out veteran? An overwhelmed system maybe? These are serious questions we should all ponder and demand solutions to.

When a veteran comes home with PTSD, a whole circle of other people also become victims and are affected. Spouses, children, relatives, and friends all bear the repercussions and often suffer secondary trauma. Way too many families are also having to experience the horrible consequences of suicide when symptoms become too unbearable for a veteran to bear, and no real structured help is available.

This also applies to the families, friends, and loved ones of all other trauma survivor groups. Isn't this completely unnecessary? If we start to piece all the healing aspects together, put our egos aside, and begin to work with one another as respectful healers, I believe all this unnecessary suffering will become something of the past. Today, however, these are the cold realities of being a trauma survivor. I think in the future we can do much better than this. Do you agree?

Now, at least, you have more information on the subject of trauma—enough to give you educated choices. In life, we are sometimes forced to experience unspeakable events that can hurt and damage us beyond anything we imagined. We can choose to stay angry, hurt, fearful and damaged, or we can use all the resources available to us to heal and rise up stronger than before. Like the phoenix rising from the ashes, we can go on with the new knowledge and understanding we've gained and continue to walk our path on the planet as extraordinary people, instead of emotionally broken people. This is the silver lining. These are the gifts trauma can bring us: deeper understanding, more compassion, and strength undefeatable.

Thrive! Be Extraordinary!

Love

When Love beckons to you, follow Him,
though His ways are hard and steep.
And when His wings enfold you yield to Him,
Though the sword hidden among his pinions may wound you.
And when He speaks to you believe in Him,
Though His voice may shatter your dreams
as the north wind lays waste the garden.
For even as Love crowns you so shall He crucify you.
Even as He is for your growth so is He for your pruning.
Even as He ascends to your height and caresses your tenderest branches
that shiver in the sun,
So shall he descend to your roots
And shake them in their clinging to the earth.
Like sheaves of corn He gathers you unto Himself.
He threshes you to make you naked.
He sifts you to free you from your husks.
He grinds you to whiteness.
He kneads you until you are pliant;
And then He assigns you to His sacred fire that you become sacred bread
For God's sacred feast.

All these things shall Love do unto you
That you may know the secrets of your heart,
And in that knowledge become a fragment of Life's heart.

But if in your fear you would seek only Love's peace and Love's pleasure,
Then it is better for you that you cover your nakedness
And pass out of Love's threshing floor,
Into the seasonless world where you shall laugh,
But not all of your laughter,
And weep,
But not all of your tears.

—Kahlil Gibran, 1883–1931, *The Prophet*, 1923

About the Author

Sharron Gleason practices Trauma Touch Healing in Carlsbad, Southern California.

She is a Certified Trauma Touch Therapist, and anyone who is seeking a consultation or is interested in receiving therapy may email her at: sgleason@traumatouchhealing.com.

Trauma Touch Healing is a new, unique and organic 12-week trauma release therapy founded by the author.
It combines Trauma Touch Therapy, Trauma Intervention, and Emotional 911 techniques which control stress, triggers, and symptoms of PTSD. Further information can be obtained from the TTH website at www.traumatouchhealing.com.

Bibliography

Keller, Helen. *The Open Door*. Garden City, NY: Doubleday, 1957.

Strieber, Whitley. *Breakthrough: The Next Step*. NY, NY: Harper Collins, 1995.

Van der Kolk, Bessel. *Psychological Trauma*. Washington, DC: American Psychiatric, 1987.

Levine, Peter A. *Waking the Tiger: Healing Trauma*. Berkeley, California: North Atlantic, 1997.

Levy-Hass, Hanna. *Inside Belsen*. Brighton, Sussex: Harvester Press, 1982.

Radha Soami Satsang Beas Society. *Spiritual Perspectives, Vol 1: Understanding the Basics*. Punjab, India: Thompson Press Ltd. (India), 2010.

Gibran, Kahlil. The Prophet. NY, NY: Alfred A. Knopf, 1939.

Hay, Louise L. *You Can Heal Your Life*. Santa Monica, Ca: Hay House, 1987.

Lazarus, Emma (1880-1968). *The New Colossus*. Sonnet written for the Statue of Liberty, 1883.

Mandela, Nelson (1918–2013). Long Walk to Freedom Speech, 1995.

Mowen, Karrie. 2001. "An Interdisciplinary Approach to Trauma." *Massage & Bodywork:* October/November 2001 Issue. Pages 29 - 36.

Smith, Chris. 1995. Professional Development. Trauma Touch Therapy. *Touchstone Journal of the Oregon Massage Technician's Association*, December 1995 Issue. Pages 14, 15, 19.